PUBLICATIONS OF THE BUREAU OF BUSINESS AND ECONOMIC RESEARCH

Recent publications in this series:

The Role of

Regional Security Exchanges

Publications of the
Bureau of Business and Economic Research
University of California

THE ROLE OF REGIONAL SECURITY EXCHANGES

BY

JAMES E. WALTER

UNIVERSITY OF CALIFORNIA PRESS
BERKELEY AND LOS ANGELES
1957

UNIVERSITY OF CALIFORNIA PRESS

BERKELEY AND LOS ANGELES

✧

CAMBRIDGE UNIVERSITY PRESS

LONDON, ENGLAND

LIBRARY OF CONGRESS CATALOG CARD NUMBER: 57-6209

BY THE UNIVERSITY OF CALIFORNIA PRINTING DEPARTMENT

Preface

The importance of efficient distribution channels for corporate securities has long been recognized. Effective markets for previously issued stocks and bonds contribute to the liquidity of such investment media and permit more widely spread ownership than would otherwise be possible. The liquidity associated with securities already in existence in turn conditions the availability of external sources of new corporate funds.

Contrary to what might be anticipated, substantial gaps exist in our knowledge of certain segments of the securities market. Recent studies by the Securities Research Unit of the Wharton School, University of Pennsylvania, under the auspices of the Merrill Foundation, tend to narrow the breach in the strategic area of over-the-counter trading, but deficiencies still remain both here and elsewhere. The consequence is that judgments of the over-all performance of distributive conduits for corporate securities must be based upon incomplete evidence.

This monograph, somewhat similar to the Wharton studies, is designed to augment the sum-total of generally available information about one or more compartments of the securities market. Attention is directed in this study to regional exchanges and their relationship with both the national exchanges and the over-the-counter channels. Unlike their affluent brethren in New York City, regional exchanges have received little consideration in investment literature.

Although description has its place, evaluation is the keynote of the succeeding discussion. At least two fundamental questions arise in connection with research into the structure of the securities market. One relates to the efficiency with which the functions assigned each subdivision are (or might be) executed. The other concerns the appropriateness of the designated tasks. Each of these aspects is afforded treatment in this study.

Despite its technical orientation, the analysis of regional exchanges can be followed by the educated layman. For those readers who are compelled to allocate their time carefully or have only a general interest in the subject, the basic premises and the gist of the argument can be obtained by perusing the first and last chapters. For others as well, some benefit may be derived from examining the concluding chapter initially.

The persons and organizations to whom acknowledgment is due are too numerous to mention in detail. The Bureau of Business and Economic Research of the University of California, Berkeley, kindly provided funds for research assistance. Ronald Kaehler, president of the San Francisco Stock Exchange, made the original records of his Exchange available and freely answered my questions, as did other officials and members of the San Francisco Exchange. Officials of other organized exchanges and executives of regional corporations also coöperated in the preparation of this monograph.

Professors W. L. Crum, M. M. Davisson, J. R. Longstreet, F. P. Morrissey, and D. A. Revzan have read parts or all of the manuscript and have offered valuable suggestions. David Eiteman, in his capacity as research assistant, did much of the statistical work. Last but not least, the helpful assistance of Professors F. L. Kidner and S. A. Mosk, past and present Directors of the Bureau of Business and Economic Research, is duly noted.

J. E. W.

Contents

issues—Over-the-counter procedures—Effect of limited publicity—Variable commissions—Dealers as principals—Compensating action by regional exchanges—Commission schedules—
Market maintenance—Volume augmentation—Other possibilities—The matter of conflicting interests

I

Introduction

Because of the preëminence of the New York and American stock exchanges, as well as that of the over-the-counter division of the securities market, regional security exchanges remain virtually unnoticed. In spite of their relative unimportance, activity on the larger regional exchanges is substantial when expressed in absolute terms. Dollar volume during 1954 approached $700,000,000 for the Midwest Exchange, as contrasted with approximately $300,-000,000 and $270,000,000 respectively for the San Francisco and Los Angeles exchanges.[1]

The area of regional security exchanges offers excellent opportunities for research not only because it has been largely ignored but for other reasons as well. First, so far as regional exchanges add to the financial strength of youthful, growing corporations by improving the marketability of outstanding shares, their contribution to economic development outweighs their worth as measured by dollar volume. Second, the present performance of regional exchanges does not necessarily reflect their potentiality. Third, the examination of regional exchanges focuses attention upon the limitations of organized security exchanges more clearly than does that of national exchanges. Fourth, the low price of memberships in regional exchanges facilitates entry into the securities field by new firms which may well provide desirable competition for well-established, nationally known brokerage firms.

PURPOSE AND PROCEDURE

The essential purpose of this study is to identify the functions of regional security exchanges and to ascertain the effectiveness with which these functions are (or might be) carried out. Regional exchanges are understood to comprise all organized security ex-

---

[1] The sources of these data are the *Annual Reports* for 1954 of the Midwest, San Francisco, and Los Angeles exchanges.

changes in the United States, except the New York and American stock exchanges and exclusively local exchanges.[2] The two New York exchanges are categorized as *national* exchanges despite the fact that the New York Stock Exchange is clearly in a class by itself. Local exchanges are defined arbitrarily as those exchanges whose dollar volume is less than one-half of 1 per cent of total dollar transactions on all organized exchanges.

The approach utilized to identify the functions of regional security exchanges is to proceed from the general to the specific. The initial step thus involves the consideration of the securities market as a unified whole and the examination of certain relevant inter-relationships among the diverse subdivisions of the securities market. Security attributes and buyer-and-seller characteristics provide the points of departure from this analysis. Our primary intention is to show where organized security exchanges fit into the scheme of things and to indicate possible areas of conflict between organized exchanges and other segments of the securities market for future reference.

The second step embraces the fabrication of a generalized framework of organized security exchanges and the enumeration of the differences between national and regional exchanges. The purpose is to isolate the avowed functions of regional exchanges and to justify the subsequent comparison—on an empirical plane—between national and regional exchanges.

Before specifying the procedure for evaluating regional exchanges, it should be observed that the meaning attached to the term "security" depends upon the context in which it is employed. As used in connection with the securities market as a whole, the concept is understood to include both credit instruments and ownership shares. As applied in connection with organized exchanges, it is construed to refer exclusively to the common and preferred stocks issued by private corporations. The reason for this distinction is simply that trading in credit instruments constitutes an insignificant part of total activity on organized exchanges.

The technique for judging the effectiveness with which the functions of regional exchanges are executed may best be described as multilateral. Consideration is given to the relative importance of regional transactions in multiply traded issues, to the comparative

---

[2] In contrast to this classification, the Securities and Exchange Commission distinguishes between *national* exchanges registered under the Securities Exchange Act of 1934 and *local* exchanges exempted from registration. Of 19 exchanges, only the Colorado Springs, Honolulu, Richmond, and Wheeling exchanges are exempted.

performance of national and regional exchanges, and to the contribution—measured in absolute terms wherever possible—of regional exchanges to the liquidity of regional stocks. Treatment of these topics is followed by an examination of the competitive advantages of over-the-counter trading.

The desirability of utilizing a four-pronged approach to the problem of evaluation arises from the intermediate position of regional security exchanges between the national exchanges and the over-the-counter area. Their connection with the national exchanges is reflected in the fact that historically they have been an important source of national listings and that they currently account for a sizable proportion of the volume in multiply traded issues in many instances. Their relation to the over-the-counter segment is shown by the fact that over-the-counter issues represent the prime source of regional listings.

The performance of regional exchanges relative to both the national exchanges and the over-the-counter area therefore possesses substantial significance to this study. Comparison with the national exchanges measures the ability of regional exchanges to minimize the loss of regional issues and their opportunity for growth through augmented activity in multiply traded issues. Comparison with the over-the-counter subdivision indicates the prospect of expansion by means of new regional listings.

The empirical tools employed to measure the performance of regional exchanges indicate their effectiveness only within the restraints imposed by historical operating procedures, trading media, securities legislation, and other factors. Since the extension of these limits may uncover unrealized potential, adequate evaluation of regional exchanges requires examination of innovations which might be introduced. With this in mind, attention is directed in the latter part of this analysis to such matters as revisions in security regulations, changes in operating procedures, and realignments among regional exchanges.

SCOPE OF ANALYSIS

Apart from the New York and American stock exchanges, only six of nineteen domestic security exchanges experienced a dollar volume which equaled or exceeded one-half of 1 per cent of total dollar transactions on all organized exchanges in 1953. Exchanges qualifying as regional, as opposed to local, exchanges on the basis of our arbitrary size criterion include the Boston, Detroit, Los

Angeles, Midwest, Philadelphia–Baltimore, and San Francisco exchanges. Although the conclusions drawn herein are believed to obtain at least in part for most regional exchanges, no attempt is made to examine each of the 6 exchanges with the same degree of thoroughness.

For reasons specified below, emphasis is placed, in the order of listing, upon the San Francisco, Los Angeles, and Midwest exchanges. Extended treatment of these exchanges is justified on the basis of over-all size and of importance of trading in regional issues. The Philadelphia–Baltimore and Boston exchanges, in contrast, are characterized by extremely high ratios of activity in multiply traded issues to total volume; the Detroit Exchange features substantially less dollar volume than any of the other 5 regional exchanges.

In a relevant sense, the San Francisco Stock Exchange may be regarded as the focal point of this study. By virtue of its remoteness from the national exchanges and its location in the heart of a rapidly growing region, the San Francisco Exchange is deemed to possess the best prospects of all regional exchanges for achieving independent status. Despite attrition in regional listings throughout the years as a result of graduation to the national exchanges, merger, and other factors, it nonetheless maintains a diversified group of regional stocks. Other considerations include the accessibility of data and the necessity of restricting the scope of the study to workable confines.

Detailed study of the San Francisco Exchange in turn involves recurring reference to the Los Angeles Exchange. The trading areas of the 2 California exchanges overlap significantly as evidenced by the presence of 19 dually traded issues. Their trading floors are linked together by direct wire facilities. The San Francisco and Los Angeles exchanges are, in addition, in the process of consolidation.

Inclusion of the Midwest Exchange data in this analysis is warranted in view of the fact that it is the largest regional exchange. The experience of the Midwest Exchange subsequent to its merger activity in 1949 may well provide useful insight into the prospects for the California exchanges. Brief treatment of the Philadelphia–Baltimore Exchange is merited on similar grounds.

SOURCES AND TREATMENT OF DATA

The area encompassed by this study is for the most part unexplored. As a consequence, primary reliance is placed upon original records and published reports of organized exchanges and upon direct communication with regional corporations and exchange officials and members.

In collecting and analyzing data, elaborate statistical techniques are avoided on the grounds that they are unnecessary and may leave misleading impressions of preciseness. Care is taken to ensure reasonable accuracy. No formal attempt is made, however, to determine either the representativeness of the opinions expressed by the corporation executives and exchange officials and members surveyed or the adequacy of the sample. Nor is every possible step taken to guarantee that the statistical data employed truly depict the status of regional exchanges. In doubtful cases, judgment, based upon the existence of satisfactory explanations, is the deciding factor.

Information about the San Francisco Stock Exchange is relatively complete. Basic records, made available for the purposes of this analysis, contain details for each stock on the daily price range and the daily volume broken down by round- and odd-lots. Daily reports record the size of individual round-lot orders and the prices at which they are executed, as well as closing bid and asked quotations. Supplementary data are obtained by means of personal interviews with the president, the vice-chairman of the Board of Governors, the chairman of the Floor Trading Committee, specialists, and other members of this exchange.

Material on other regional exchanges is noticeably less comprehensive. Correspondence with exchange officials, together with annual reports and yearly summaries of transactions, constitutes the principal source of information. The result is that interesting questions remain unanswered in some instances and the generality of our conclusions is not wholly confirmed.

Usable statistics on the over-the-counter segment are virtually nonexistent. The Securities Research Unit of the Wharton School, University of Pennsylvania, has recently published a series of monographs on this subject under the auspices of the Merrill Foundation. Unfortunately, however, these studies are not designed to provide the kind of data requisite to this analysis. The absence of specific information on activity in individual over-the-counter issues and other items forces us to speak in general terms and to rely heavily upon surveys of sample groups of "listed" and "over-the-counter" corporations.

A variety of other sources are employed throughout this study. The *Wall Street Journal* reports on realignments among regional exchanges and revisions in their operating procedures and publishes both prices and transactions in listed securities and closing bid and asked quotations in untraded listings. Hearings on the stock market before the Senate Committee on Banking and Currency (Eighty-fourth Congress, First Session) include statements by the presidents of the Midwest and San Francisco exchanges and contain other relevant data. Reference is also made to the *Year Book* of the New York Stock Exchange, to the annual reports of the national exchanges, and to special studies and reports prepared by both the national and regional exchanges.

OTHER CONSIDERATIONS

Before proceeding with the analysis proper, two points should be raised concerning the orientation of this study. One is that the order of importance attached herein to the functions of regional exchanges does not appear to coincide with that assigned by the members of regional exchanges. The other is that, *ceteris paribus,* organized exchanges are presumed to be more suitable market places for the trading of qualified stocks than is the over-the-counter segment of the securities market.

In ranking exchange functions, the position is taken that the basic function of regional exchanges should be to service regional issues. As is demonstrated subsequently, it is difficult to justify the continued existence of regional exchanges on other grounds. Although members of regional exchanges pay homage to this consideration, their primary attention appears to be devoted to augmenting regional activity in multiply traded issues.[3]

With respect to the preference shown for organized exchanges, the opinion is held that the listing of stocks for which organized exchanges can provide satisfactory markets benefits the investor group as a whole. Full disclosure of transactions reduces the opportunity for discrimination among investors. Exchange requirements for periodic and detailed reporting by corporations in turn allows investment decisions to be based more upon observed fact than speculative fantasy.

---

[3] See, for example, the pamphlet, entitled *San Francisco Stock Exchange, 1955,* in which exclusive consideration is given to the regional listing of nationally listed issues.

II

Identification of Regional Exchange Functions

Evaluation of either the present or the potential performance of regional security exchanges presupposes reasonably precise specification of that which is to be measured. The initial task—to which this chapter is devoted—thus becomes one of ascertaining what it is that regional exchanges are supposed to accomplish.

If regional security exchanges are but components of *the* securities market, an appropriate point of departure to the problem of isolating regional exchange functions is the securities market itself.[1] The procedure employed consists, first, of rationalizing the existing arrangement of the securities market in order to ascertain the specialized role of organized security exchanges and, then, of differentiating between national and regional exchanges. Advantages accruing from this line of attack include the early introduction of useful concepts and the disclosure of interrelationships which are fundamental to the subsequent analysis.

An alternative method utilized to supplement the basic development is simply to record the opinions of exchange members and executives of corporations whose shares are listed regionally. This approach is deficient in that the attitudes of those surveyed are conditioned by short-run, personal considerations. The thinking of the officials and members of regional exchanges and of corporation executives is nonetheless relevant for they, acting in their decision-making capacities, determine the future of regional exchanges to an appreciable extent.

---

[1] Queries may be raised as to whether the securities market is not in reality a collection of closely connected markets. The answer to this question, as might be expected, is largely a matter of judgment. The fact that the objective in owning securities of all types is, with minor exceptions, fundamentally the same, favors the one-market view. The fact that securities are, for one reason or another, often imperfectly substitutive may favor the opposing view.

In an over-all sense, the securities market exists to facilitate the transfer of claims to income.[2] Individual compartments of the securities market may be said to have purpose, that is, to possess specialized functions to the extent that their continued operation contributes to the underlying objective. The mere fact that subdivisions exist is not to be taken as conclusive evidence of their intrinsic worth. Nor should the current emphasis of any given segment of the market be accepted without question as the proper basis for judging the role of this subdivision in the future.

FACTORS INFLUENCING THE MAKE-UP OF THE SECURITIES MARKET

Major determinants of the characteristics of distribution channels ordinarily include both the nature of the asset class and the composition and number of buyers and sellers. The further constraint of government regulation is often superimposed wherever the net result of market forces fails to satisfy social standards. Application of these general considerations to the securities market implies that items worthy of investigation comprise the attributes of securities, the make-up of security holders, and the degree of (and basis for) regulation.

SECURITY ATTRIBUTES

The fact that *securities* are essentially claims to future income and, unlike real property, have no utility in themselves warrant their treatment as a distinctive asset class.[3] The fact that the size, time-shape, and certainty of future income flows vary widely among securities justifies the erection of subcategories within the securities group. When associated with the diverse kinds of security holders, these subdivisions may well explain the existence of multiple distribution channels.

Features common to most securities include negligible costs of holding, ready transferability, and the absence of tangible differ-

---

[2] Ownership of securities permits, in some instances, control of the underlying wealth. Since securities held for this purpose are rarely traded and may be regarded as indirect titles to property, however, the claim-to-income aspect is emphasized.

[3] Repayments of principal, for which provision is made in the case of credit instruments, are viewed as elements of future income. The validity of this treatment is demonstrated by the fact that both interest and principal payments determine the present value (V_p) of limited-life securities, i.e.,

$$V_p = \frac{C}{1+i} + \frac{C}{(1+i)^2} + \cdots + \frac{C+P}{(1+i)}n,$$

where C is the coupon rate, P is the amount of principal repayment, and i is the capitalization rate.

ences between new and used (in the sense of previously issued) securities. Negligible holding costs render securities excellent trading media and facilitate speculative activity. Securities neither deteriorate through time in the usual meaning of the word, nor require elaborate storage facilities.[4] So far as securities are registered by the issuer in the name of the owner or his representative, insurance and other safety precautions are unnecessary. As items of personal property, securities are, in addition, subjected to relatively light taxation.

Ready transferability further enhances the value of securities as trading media. For this and other reasons implied in the nature of the asset class, security holders operate in dual capacities with equal facility. They are prepared in many instances to buy and/or sell securities, often at a moment's notice, provided the price is right.

Distinctions between new and previously issued securities, to the extent that they exist, arise in connection with the relative size of individual offerings and the type of seller. The dollar amount of a new issue normally exceeds that of the typical resale transaction by a wide margin. Although this difference is essentially one of degree, it may well indicate the need for specialized procedures to effect the distribution of new issues.

Recipients of proceeds from the sale of new securities are the issuing agencies, as opposed to members of the investing public in the event of resale transactions. Despite the fact that sale of either new or currently outstanding securities represents a source of funds to the seller, it follows from the character of issuing organizations that new offerings are more likely to be associated with physical investment and productive effort. The purposes for which proceeds are employed do not, however, directly affect the structure of the securities market.

Other things being equal, the purchaser cares little whether the security acquired is new or used. The consequence is that the new issue market is little more than a subdivision of the market for existing securities. By virtue of their numerical superiority, measured in either physical or dollar terms, and of their objective price histories, old securities determine in large part the prices of new offerings and condition their acceptability.

Of equal significance to the foregoing security characteristics is the intragroup diversity occasioned by variations in the char-

---

[4] As employed in this context, the term "deteriorate" refers to physical impairment attributable to the passage of time; it does not encompass fluctuations in security prices even though they may reflect changes in the character of the underlying wealth.

acter of, and risk associated with, the future income streams to which securities have claim. Both the character of income flows and the degree of risk attached thereto are influenced by the type of issuer, the status of the claim to income, governmental action, and other less important factors. Securities may be issued by a wide variety of public and private agencies and may possess creditor, residual (ownership), or hybrid status.[5]

Legislative or administrative action by government operates in devious ways. For United States government securities, guaranteed repurchase and price-support policies, carried out by the Federal Reserve System, appreciably augment liquidity. For state and local government issues, the tax-free nature of their income exerts a noticeable influence on yields. In other instances, the existence of legal lists for institutions and trusts and of preferential tax treatment for capital gains differentiate the affected issues from the normal run of securities. Each of these disturbs the yield-risk relationship in one fashion or another.

Intraclass differences are reflected in the wide range of prices at which securities are offered for sale. The large assortment of prices obtains primarily from differences in the degree of risk, as associated with given yields, and from the fact that ownership interest can be partitioned almost without limit through the authorization and issuance of additional shares. In similar fashion, credit instruments are made available in many denominations.

The combined effect of this diversity is to produce a variety of security subdivisions. At one extreme are money substitutes, comprising short-term government bonds for the most part; at the opposite end of the scale are highly risky common shares issued by small, weakly financed ventures. To the extent that each subgroup satisfies specific and unique requirements and/or is possessed primarily by one class (or a very few) of security holders, intracategory variations among securities are likely to give rise to a number of heterogeneous, but interrelated, marketing avenues.

COMPOSITION OF SECURITY HOLDERS

Although exhaustive treatment of the composition of security holders is unnecessary, two aspects are especially relevant to this analysis. One concerns the coexistence of large and small investors. The other pertains to the tendency for certain investor groups to emphasize particular types of securities.

[5] Examples of hybrid status include preferred stocks and convertible creditor instruments.

Let us suppose—with some degree of realism—that partitioning by *institutions* and *individuals* differentiates adequately between large and small security holders. The size of institutional portfolios implies that decisions by this group to buy or sell securities may exert a noticeable impact upon the prices of the securities in question. So far as this result obtains, the perfection of the securities market is impaired, and the auction type of trading fails to function properly.

Institutions, as opposed to individuals, are inclined to invest heavily in a relatively few security subclasses. As a rule, banks and nonfinancial corporations stress government securities. Life insurance companies rely heavily upon high-grade debt instruments. Pension funds and investment companies invest in ownership shares, but still emphasize quality for the most part. Although the preferences of individuals cover the entire range with the possible exception of high-grade corporate bonds, individuals can nonetheless be classified in accordance with variations in portfolio requirements.[6]

The large individual holdings of institutions encourage negotiated over-the-counter trading and, in the case of life insurance companies, direct placement of new issues. The fact that debt instruments are favored institutional investments suggests that securities of this type will be traded on negotiated, rather than auction, bases. To the extent that ownership shares are held by institutions, the same conclusion applies.

The influence of individuals upon the character of the securities market is quite different. Not only is the average size of security holdings by individuals small, but institutions are, numerically speaking, overwhelmed by individuals. Some 8,630,000 individuals spread throughout the United States are estimated to own common stock, as contrasted with life insurance companies which total 793 and commercial and savings banks which number 14,422.[7]

These considerations affect the marketing of securities held by individuals (other than purely defensive holdings) in two ways. Since security holders function with equal facility as buyers or sellers, active trading of the auction type is encouraged. For the channel(s) through which securities held by individuals are dis-

---

[6] Although bank-administered trusts for individuals may occupy an intermediate position, they are considered to belong to this latter category.

[7] Sources of these data include *Who Owns American Business?* (New York: New York Stock Exchange, 1956), p. 5; *Life Insurance Fact Book* (New York: Institute of Life Ins., 1954), p. 44; and *Federal Reserve Bulletin*, XXXX, no. 12 (Dec., 1954), p. 1269.

tributed to approach perfection, however, intermediate agencies must exist to collect buy-and-sell orders and centralize trading activity.

The numerical importance of individuals as security holders and the small average size of their holdings constitute a prime reason for government regulation of the securities market. The typical individual possesses neither the knowledge nor the resources to ascertain without assistance the true facts about any security. Although private agencies can satisfy needs of this type, they frequently await the initial push by government. Once adopted, government regulation in turn shapes the character of the market.

To illustrate, several effects of government regulation upon the securities market are readily discernible. In establishing minimum-size requirements for the registration of new issues, government regulation often conditions the size of new issues. In differentiating between listed and unlisted securities, government regulation influences decisions to list and thus the relative significance of different marketing channels. In restricting the investment banking operations of commercial banks to Governments and Municipals, a mutiplicity of distribution channels for securities is promoted.

ORGANIZATION OF THE SECURITIES MARKET

The structure of the securities market which has evolved throughout the years appears consistent with the parameters set by the nature of securities, by the composition and number of security holders, and by government regulation. The existing market structure cannot, however, be viewed as the only possible structure; nor can it be accepted without further question as the best of all possible structures.

A FLOW CHART

Figure 1 depicts, in highly condensed form, the prevailing organization of the securities market. Orders to buy and to sell securities are initiated by individuals and institutions. In the case of new securities, orders to sell originate with the issuing agency. With certain exceptions, these orders are transmitted to brokerage houses which, depending upon the security involved and related considerations, serve either as intermediaries (i.e., agents) or as principals.[8]

The significance of intermediaries declines sharply wherever direct or private placement is concerned and whenever large institutions, as distinct from individuals, acquire or dispose of securities. Under direct placement, the issuing agency deals directly with the buyer (ordinarily life insurance companies), and the investment banker at best has only an advisory function. Pressure for direct negotiation by life insurance companies arises principally

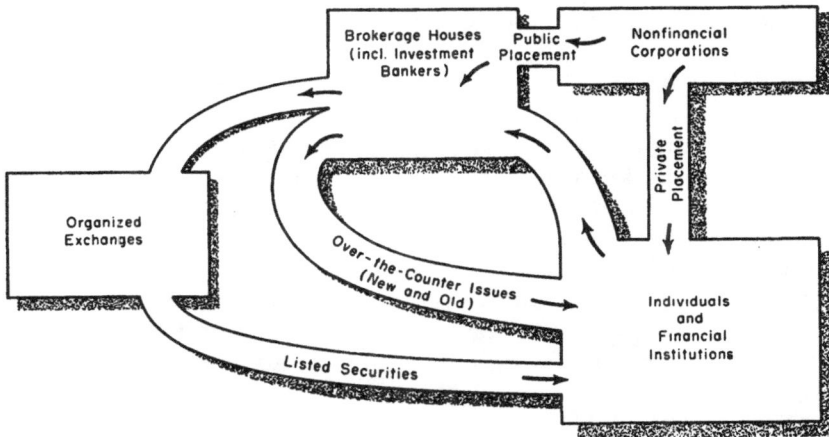

Fig. 1. A flow chart of corporate securities.

from the size of their investment requirements and their ability to absorb sizable issues individually. Because of their specialized personnel and substantial holdings, moreover, large financial and nonprofit institutions are able, if they so desire, to perform many of the buying and selling functions normally assigned to brokerage houses.

To facilitate resale transactions in widely dispersed ownership shares, broker associations—designated as organized exchanges— have been established and have existed for many years.[9] At the end of 1953, 1,530 stock issues were listed on the New York Stock Exchange, as compared with 503 issues listed on the American

[8] In view of the fact that dealers in securities often carry on a variety of activities, the term "brokerage house or firm" is considered to include investment banking, as well as other functions.

[9] The New York Stock Exchange, for example, was founded in 1792.

Stock Exchange.[10] In addition, some 305 issues were admitted to unlisted trading privileges on the American Stock Exchange. Other issues listed on regional exchanges may number as many as 1,276. With certain exceptions, these constitute the better-known stocks and are broadly distributed throughout the trading areas of the exchanges in question.

Organized exchanges serve as focal points for trading in listed stocks. Normal-sized orders in these stocks are forwarded by the brokerage houses to the floor of the exchanges and executed.[11] Large-sized orders to buy or sell listed issues are, in contrast, frequently executed off the exchange floor in order to avoid undue price disturbances.

As might be anticipated from the importance of institutional holdings of debt instruments, organized exchanges do not serve as focal points for trading in high grade, listed corporate bonds. In terms of market values, the ratio of bonds traded on the New York Stock Exchange during 1953 to listed bonds outstanding amounted to less than 1 per cent, as contrasted with a ratio which approximated 12 per cent for listed stocks.[12] Since institutions own the bulk of corporate bonds, negotiated trading has certain advantages, such as lower costs for large transactions and limited publicity, which are not presently offered by the auction-type organized exchange.

Components of the securities market, other than the organized exchanges, are commonly referred to as *over-the-counter markets.* Over-the-counter markets encompass the distribution channels for federal, state, and muncipial securities, and unlisted stocks, as well as for those items already indicated. These divisions are characterized by secrecy, flexibility, and active broker-dealer participation.

In over-the-counter trading, individual brokerage firms make the markets for the different securities and actively promote these issues. Orders to buy or to sell over-the-counter are thus executed by the original recipient or forwarded to another brokerage firm which has become recognized as a primary market for the security in question.[13] Except where the dealer acts as agent, the spread

---

[10] New York Stock Exchange, *1954 Year Book,* p. 22; American Stock Exchange, *President's Report,* 1953–1954, p. 22.

[11] By "normal-sized" is meant orders not exceeding a few hundred shares, except in the case of low-priced (e.g., $1–$10) issues.

[12] New York Stock Exchange, *1954 Year Book,* pp. 22, 23, and 35.

[13] Information of this type is available from the National Quotation Bureau.

between "bid" and "asked" prices constitutes the profit margin.

Brokerage firms ordinarily confine their attention neither to special classes of securities nor to particular distribution channels. The major instance of specialization arises in connection with federal, state, and municipal bonds. For these securities, the total volume of trading and the average size per transaction are such that opportunity exists for increasing returns to scale. Legislative restrictions upon the investment banking and other brokerage functions of commercial banks, together with the utilization of United States government securities as a prime instrument of effecting monetary policy, further foster the development of specialized dealers in this area.

RELATION BETWEEN ORGANIZED EXCHANGES AND OVER-THE-COUNTER MARKETING CHANNELS

Of particular pertinence to this study is the relation between organized exchanges and the over-the-counter area. Conclusions concerning the functions of regional security exchanges depend to a considerable extent upon the effectiveness of over-the-counter channels in distributing ownership shares. With this in mind, the foregoing sketch of the securities market is extended to cover, in brief fashion, factors contributing to the success of the over-the-counter division of the securities market. The case for organized exchanges is presented in the succeeding section.

The adaptability of over-the-counter procedures to the specific requirements of different security classes constitutes the principal longer-run basis for effective competition with organized exchanges in the marketing of ownership shares. Incentives, that is, spreads, are adjusted in accordance with the size of individual transactions, selling effort, risk, and other considerations. The consequence of this flexibility is, among other things, that regional corporations whose shares are not broadly held and whose names are not widely publicized have strong inducement for their issues to be traded over-the-counter.

Perhaps the strategic factor influencing the choice of distribution channels in the short run is the brokerage house itself. Although brokerage firms as a group may benefit from additional listings and increased activity on organized exchanges, individual houses lose the advantages of vested interests. That is to say, the opportunity for monopoly profits is often greater in the over-the-counter area than on the organized exchanges. The fact that new issues have traditionally been marketed over-the-counter also exerts a substantial influence. If the selling organization created to handle new issues is to be utilized fully and continuously, trading in new issues must often be supplemented by the retailing of previously issued securities.

Other considerations affecting the selection of marketing channels include government regulation and management attitudes toward speculative activity. With respect to regulation, distinction is made between corporations whose shares are listed and those whose shares are not. Companies whose shares are listed on organized exchanges are required to submit periodic reports to the Securities and Exchange Commission. With respect to management attitudes, the relatively high degree of speculation on organized exchanges apparently deters many firms from listing their securities. Few banks, for example, have their shares listed for this very reason.

The degree to which over-the-counter markets justifiably impinge upon organized exchanges is not obvious from these remarks. It may nonetheless be said that the volume of stocks currently traded over-the-counter is probably greater than is economically warranted.

STRUCTURE OF ORGANIZED SECURITY EXCHANGES

For analytic purposes, organized exchanges can be broken down into the national exchanges located in New York City, and the regional exchanges dispersed throughout the United States. Of these two groups, the national exchanges are presently by far the most important. In terms of share volume, the New York and American stock exchanges accounted for approximately 88 per cent of the aggregate activity on registered exchanges during 1953.[14]

Whatever their size, organized security exchanges are typically patterned after the principal exchange, that is, the New York Stock Exchange. Uniform procedures and commission rates are normally applied without reference to the specific characteristics of the security traded. In view of this similarity of pattern and uniformity of procedures, it appears feasible to consider initially the general character of organized security exchanges.

This approach is not intended to convey the impression that

---

[14] Securities and Exchange Commission, *Statistical Bulletin.*

the problems confronting national and regional exchanges are identical. Reasons exist for believing that substantial differences are present. If so, an interesting question arises as to whether the similarity of pattern and of commission rates is indeed consistent with the peculiar requirements of regional exchanges.

THE BASIC PATTERN

Stripped of their vestment, organized security exchanges are little more than collection places for orders to buy and sell securities. Thus exchanges do not differ markedly from other segments of the securities market, except perhaps in the type of security traded and in the trader. It is through their organization and formalized procedures that organized exchanges achieve sufficient uniqueness to merit separate treatment.

Apart from syndicate operations in connection with new issues and secondary distributions, organized exchanges represent the most highly developed form of group endeavor in the marketing of securities. Organized exchanges are at once joint marketing ventures and regulatory agencies. This combination of functions occasions rigidities which apparently condition the potentiality of the exchanges.

The joint marketing feature arises from the fact that orders to buy and sell securities flow into the exchanges through member firms. Buy orders are paired off against sell orders on the floors of the exchanges by members, designated as specialists, on a first-come, first-served basis. Limited orders away from market and of varying duration, together with short and long positions taken by specialists in their function as market stabilizers, reduce the amplitude of short-term price changes.

The regulatory feature is attributable to the sensitive nature of the securities market. The typical investor is in no position to judge the validity of financial data disclosed to him. He is vulnerable to both "insider" operations and unscrupulous salesmen.

So far as organized exchanges fail to regulate member activities and to establish adequate reporting standards for corporations which list their securities, government agencies assume these functions. The Securities and Exchange Commission has occupied this stand-by role since 1934.

Membership in organized exchanges is limited in varying degrees. This restriction in members is both a cause and an effect of regulation. It is a cause in the sense that uncontrolled monopolistic privileges are likely to be abused.[15] It is an effect in the sense that regulation is simplified if the participants are few in number and have financial inducements to conform.

Largely, though not entirely, because of their regulatory function and of the nature of federal securities regulation, organized security exchanges do not readily adapt selling procedures to fit the different security classes except in a very general fashion. Broad distinctions are made between stocks and bonds, active and inactive securities, and round- and odd-lots. Commission rates, as applied to stocks, vary inversely with the size of the transaction up to and including 100-share limits. For transactions which are multiples of 100 shares, the rate decreases as the price of the security increases.

Apart from differences of this character, uniformity of treatment prevails for the most part. Common registration and reporting standards apply to all corporations whose securities are listed. No provision exists for publicizing the less known companies, other than the daily reporting of prices and volume. Nor are facilities available on the organized exchanges for soliciting orders wherever the volume is inadequate. In addition, the positions which specialists are required to be able to assume in carrying out their market stabilization function are extremely limited and are unrelated to the requirements of individual securities.[16]

It follows that organized exchanges are designed to service only a few types of securities, namely, those whose merchandising needs happen to correspond with exchange procedures. Based upon the preceding comments, the ideal security for listing on organized exchanges appears to have the following trading characteristics. The issuing company should be well-known throughout the trading area, and its securities widely held. The volume of transactions for each security should be substantial, but the dollar magnitude of each transaction relatively small.

In view of the differentiation between round and odd lots, the security's price—for common shares—should probably be substan-

---

[15] Note, however, that discrimination in over-the-counter markets resulting from imperfect knowledge may be fully as significant as any abuses of monopolistic privileges which are likely to occur on organized exchanges.

[16] The New York Stock Exchange requires that each specialist have sufficient capital to purchase 400 shares of each stock assigned to him. The San Francisco Exchange requires each specialist to have resources equal to one-half the market value of a "board" lot for all stocks assigned to him or funds adequate to meet a margin requirement amounting to 30 per cent of his position, whichever is higher.

tially below $100.[17] In view of registration and reporting require-
ments, as well as for reasons already given, the issuing company
should be sizable.

Securities which do not possess these qualities may still be listed.
For them, the effectiveness of organized exchanges as marketing
channels is less than ideal, and decisions to list securities must
represent compromises. The crucial question becomes whether or
not other segments of the securities market exist which satisfy more
nearly the selling requirements of these securities. It is at this point
that the flexibility of over-the-counter trading registers with such
telling effect.

POSITION OF REGIONAL SECURITY EXCHANGES

Cursory examination of the securities market has revealed that
organized security exchanges provide a relatively specialized channel for marketing certain kinds of ownership shares. The question
now arises as to the specific contribution of regional security exchanges. The answer presumably hinges upon the proposition that
the issuing corporations should be well-known throughout the trading area of the exchange upon which its stocks are listed.

Despite the fact that many issues are multiply traded on national
and regional security exchanges, let us suppose initially that the
overlapping of functions is unwarranted. It follows that the stocks
of nationally known companies should be traded on the New York
exchanges, whereas those of regionally known corporations are
appropriate for regional exchanges.[18] The supporting argument
most frequently propounded is simply that regional securities receive inadequate attention when listed with the national exchanges.

Contributions of regional security exchanges to the liquidity of
regional issues are likely to be less impressive than the corresponding benefits accruing to nationally listed shares for at least one
reason. The fortunes of regional corporations are often closely associated with the economic conditions prevailing within the respective trading areas of their securities. Decisions by shareholders to
augment liquidity may thus occur at the very time when the earn-
nings expectations of regional companies are poor. The consequence is that price and volume fluctuations in regionally held

---

[17] This point is, however, qualified by the fact that commissions currently discriminate against low-priced issues.

[18] See, for example, R. Thorson, "The Midwest Stock Exchange," *Analysts Journal*,
X, no. 1 (Feb., 1954), pp. 57–59.

and listed securities may be relatively greater than in nationally distributed and listed securities.[19]

The force of this point varies directly with the economic strength and diversity of the trading area encompassed by any given regional exchange. It is conceivable that, if the fragmentation is not excessive, a part may exhibit the same characteristics as the whole.

Even if the New York and outlying exchanges were adjudged equally effective, the problem of adequate volume to justify the existence of the latter still arises. A sufficient number of regional corporations which meet the desired specifications may simply not exist. It is possible that company growth curves are such that the duration for which securities are suitable for listing on regional exchanges is relatively brief.

To illustrate, let us assume that the typical growth curve for corporations which survive the initial struggle for existence is S-shaped. Before the period of rapid growth, the stock of such companies may be best adapted to over-the-counter trading. The reason is essentially that sales of the securities in question must be actively promoted. Soon after the growth commences, the stock becomes eligible for national listing. Under these conditions, management may well conclude that regional listing cannot be justified.

The matter of sufficient volume is complicated by direct competition between regional exchanges and over-the-counter markets. Since a sizable proportion of their income accrues from over-the-counter trading in regionally known securities, brokerage houses are naturally reluctant to have them listed. This factor, taken in conjunction with the inflexibilities and lack of prestige which characterize regional exchanges, undoubtedly curtails the number of new listings on regional exchanges.

If the volume of trading on regional listings is insufficient, regional security exchanges must resort to multiple listings.[20] The ratio of trading in multiple listings to total activity on regional exchanges thus becomes a partial measure of the economic justification for regional exchanges. Low ratios imply self-sufficiency; whereas high ratios suggest that the securities market may be unduly splintered.

Contrary to our initial presumption, regional trading in nationally listed stocks may serve a limited purpose by diminishing the

---

[19] See, for example, figure 2 in which a price index of leading issues traded primarily on the San Francisco Exchange is contrasted with that of Moody's.

[20] The term "multiple listing" refers to securities which are listed and/or traded on both national and regional exchanges.

force of one possible censure of national security exchanges. This criticism relates to the difficulty of entry and the likelihood of monopoly profits. James E. Day, president of the Midwest Exchange, testified before the Senate Committee on Banking and Currency:[21]

... as long as we are able to deal in the stock that they (the New York Stock Exchange) deal in and we can providing there are security listings—and a very fine means has been provided by the Securities and Exchange Commission for applying for what we call unlisted trading privileges— ... , I cannot see question of monopoly.

The high price of membership on the New York Stock Exchange precludes the participation of small brokerage firms in the markets serviced by this exchange unless such alternatives as regional exchanges exist. By virtue of low-priced memberships and multiple trading, the existence of regional exchanges enables small brokerage agencies to compete on relatively equal terms with large firms and to obtain commissions on the execution of orders in national listings. The anticipated benefit of low-cost entry and numerous participants is the competitive pricing of services offered by brokerage firms.

In actual fact, the effect of easy entry upon pricing policy appears thus far to have been indirect. As evidenced by the willingness of regional exchanges to adopt the commission schedules established by the New York Stock Exchange, the condition is one of price leadership. So far as it exists, competition is of the nonprice variety. Acceptance of this situation is reflected in the testimony of Mr. Day before the Senate Banking Committee.[22]

Whether *ease of entry* should be viewed as a supplementary function of regional exchanges is a matter of judgment. The position taken herein is that the problem can be resolved by simpler means and is therefore of doubtful relevance to this discussion.

FLEXIBILITY OF EXCHANGE PROCEDURES

Considerable stress has been placed upon the observed rigidity of organized exchange procedures. Despite recent innovations (noted in subsequent chapters) introduced by regional exchanges, the fact remains that uniformities overshadow procedural differences. Whether inflexibility is an inherent characteristic is a matter of

---

[21] *Hearings on Factors Affecting the Buying and Selling of Equity Securities,* 84th Cong., 1st sess. (Washington, 1955), pp. 194–195.

[22] *Ibid.,* p. 195.

some importance to this analysis in view of the concern over the prospective, as well as present, performance of regional exchanges.

The relatively limited range of variation in the procedures of domestic exchanges does not necessarily imply that such need be the case. As collection places for orders to buy and sell common shares, organized exchanges can conceivably exhibit a number of different operating arrangements. Significant and unavoidable rigidities are confined to those which arise from the existence of the Securities and Exchange Commission and the associated efforts of organized exchanges to regulate the activities of members.

To illustrate the potential flexibility of organized exchanges, brief reference is made to the Toronto Stock Exchange. The procedures employed by this leading Canadian exchange reflect its emphasis upon the speculative shares of oil and mining companies. Although stocks are assigned to definite posts on the Toronto trading floor, specialists are not provided to maintain continuous markets. Traders who first place bids at the highest bid prices or offers at the lowest offer prices are entitled to hold the market for ten board lots. Trading rules prescribed by the Toronto Exchange do little more in this connection than to prescribe minimum spreads between quotations, to specify that representatives of the same member firm may not trade simultaneously in a given stock, and to provide a watch-dog committee.

The absence of specialists apparently does not adversely affect trading volume. As indicated subsequently, annual share turnover for the Toronto Exchange exceeds that for both the New York and American exchanges. W. L. Somerville, assistant general manager of the Toronto Exchange states in correspondence that:

It is true that trading in this manner does not, perhaps, provide as steady a market as in markets maintaining specialist trading but it is difficult to understand how specialist trading, as it is known on the New York and American Stock Exchanges, could be maintained in speculative securities of mining and oil companies which are subject to fluctuations of considerable extent . . .

At least two other features of the Toronto Exchange are also of interest. The size of board lots varies inversely with the security's price. For mining shares selling under $1.00, the board lot is 500 shares, as contrasted to 100 shares for securities whose price equals or exceeds $1.00. For other securities, the board lot ranges from 100 shares for securities selling under $25 to 10 shares for those whose price equals or exceeds $100.

In a similar fashion, minimum commission schedules established by this and other Canadian exchanges penalize transactions in low-priced issues less severely than do domestic commission schedules. Commission rates, in addition, lack uniformity between security classes. Brokerage charges for the execution of board-lot orders in mining and oil securities whose share prices are below $20 range from one-fifth to one-half less than those imposed upon transactions in industrial securities falling within corresponding price categories.

Comparisions of Canadian and domestic commission charges, shown in table 1, are based upon the official scales of commissions for the Vancouver and New York stock exchanges. The Vancouver rates parallel those imposed by the eastern Canadian exchanges. In accord with the emphasis of most Canadian exchanges, low-priced, speculative media receive relatively preferential treatment thereon. For high-priced issues, commission rates set by exchanges in the United States are generally lower.[23]

The case study of the Toronto Exchange serves to demonstrate that domestic security exchanges undoubtedly possess some degree of latent flexibility. Faint though they may be, recent deviations from the norm by regional exchanges substantiate this conclusion. The implication is that regional exchanges may well not have reached the end of their resources for attracting regional issues.

CONCLUSIONS CONCERNING THE FUNCTIONS OF REGIONAL EXCHANGES

In essence, the basic function of any organized security exchange appears to be the efficient marketing of ownership shares, including preferred stocks, which are widely dispersed and well-known throughout the trading area encompassed by the exchange. A variety of subsidiary and/or dependent functions may be substituted for this underlying one. Reference has been made to the regulatory aspect of organized security exchanges, as well as to their disclosure requirements. A survey of "regionally listed" corporations, described subsequently, directs attention to the impact of listing upon share distribution, marketability, ease of new financing, prestige, and good will. Although not developed at this point, these considerations are treated as the occasion arises.

---

[23] Note, however, the small board lots for high-priced Toronto industrial listings. As a result of differences in board or round lots, conclusions drawn from these comparisons are subject to qualification.

TABLE 1

COMPARISON OF MINIMUM COMMISSION RATES ON CANADIAN
AND DOMESTIC EXCHANGES

Assumed price per share	Board-lot commissions, expressed as percentage of market price		
	Canadian mining and oil listings	Canadian industrial listings	New York exchange listings
$ 1.00.........................	2.0	4.0	6.0
3.00.........................	1.7	2.7	2.7
5.00.........................	2.0	3.0	2.0
10.00.........................	2.0	2.5	1.5
20.00.........................	1.5	1.5	1.3
50.00.........................	.8	.8	.8
100.00.........................	.6	.6	.5
200.00.........................	.5	.5	.3

SOURCE: New York and Vancouver Stock exchanges.

TABLE 2

RELATIONSHIP OF SHARE VOLUME IN MULTIPLY TRADED ISSUES TO TOTAL VOLUME[a]—
7 REGIONAL EXCHANGES
(in per cent)

Exchanges	1953	1952	1948	1944
Boston......................	85.0	83.5	82.8	64.2
Detroit......................	69.6	69.2	56.6	38.7
Los Angeles.................	37.1	41.6	38.8	43.2
Midwest[b]..................	69.8	69.3	62.1	49.6
Philadelphia-Baltimore[c].......	91.7	91.6	89.2	83.5
Pittsburgh..................	54.3	46.5	49.8	43.0
San Francisco...............	27.4	25.5	36.9	39.5
Total....................	54.4	54.0	53.7	50.3

SOURCE: Department of Research and Statistics, New York Stock Exchange.
[a] As reported to S.E.C.
[b] Data for 1944 and 1948 include Chicago and Cleveland Stock exchanges.
[c] Data for 1944 and 1948 include Philadelphia Stock Exchange only.

The primary function of regional security exchanges may be said to differ from that of national exchanges by virtue of the restricted trading areas which characterize regional exchanges. Regional exchanges can effectively service regional issues which do not qualify for national listing for one reason or another. Although able to provide satisfactory markets for nationally distributed stocks, regional exchanges are not equipped to take the place of national exchanges.[24]

Opinions expressed by members of the San Francisco Exchange, and substantiated by the relative importance of regional trading in nationally listed issues, nonetheless suggest that the servicing of regional issues is no longer considered to be the foremost function of regional exchanges. The prevalent attitude seems to be that regional exchanges are quasi-independent branches of the New York exchanges. If such is the case, their essential function must be one of permitting regional (small) brokerage firms entry into a field from which they would otherwise be excluded.

The permanence of this latter function is subject to question. It depends upon the continuation of exclusive tactics on the part of the national exchanges. Members of regional exchanges admit that this function could be eliminated by the simple expedient of the New York exchanges offering reasonable discounts on commission rates to nonmember firms which originate business. In the event that the encroachment of regional exchanges on the preserves of the national exchanges continues to increase, this step may well be taken.

Because of the tenuous basis upon which the function of facilitating entry rests, emphasis is placed herein upon the ability of regional exchanges to provide acceptable markets for regional issues. The fact that this aspect is stressed does not deny the possibility that regional trading in national listings offers certain advantages. Granted the desirability of national exchanges, however, the benefits of multiple trading—if they exist—must at some point be offset by the unfortunate consequences of excessive market splitting.

[24] It is of course conceivable that regional exchanges alone could perform the function of national exchanges, provided mutual trading arrangements were established and direct wire facilities connected the regional exchanges.

III

Measuring the Effectiveness of Regional Exchanges

Attention has thus far been directed to an examination of the component parts of the securities market. The conclusion drawn is that the most promising activity ascribable to regional security exchanges is that of providing acceptable markets for regional issues. The pertinent question now becomes whether regional exchanges effectively perform this function.

At least three alternative procedures can be employed to evaluate regional exchanges. One method, as suggested previously, is simply to examine the ratios of trading in multiply listed securities to total activity for the leading regional exchanges.[1] Another is to utilize the New York exchanges as bases for comparison. This approach presupposes that the New York exchanges are comparable to regional exchanges in certain relevant respects, and are in some sense ideal. Still another—and by far the most difficult—is to formulate absolute criteria for judgment. These alternatives are considered in the order of listing and are supplemented by a comparison of over-the-counter trading and trading on regional exchanges.

REGIONAL TRADING IN NATIONAL LISTINGS

Utilization of multiple-trading ratios to measure the effectiveness of regional exchanges is complicated by the refusal of the New York exchanges to permit discounts on commission charges to nonmember firms which originate business. Regional brokerage firms— much the same as their national counterparts—must recommend and accept orders to buy or sell national as well as regional listings

[1] The term "multiply listed" is used herein as if it were synonymous with "multiply traded." It should be observed, however, that many issues receive "unlisted trading privileges" and may be multiply traded even though listed on only one exchange.

if clientele accounts are to be serviced adequately. In the absence of reasonable discounts, they are compelled to rely upon reciprocity and multiple trading or override fees for income from transactions in nationally listed issues.

From the standpoint of regional brokerage firms, multiple trading possesses distinct advantages over reciprocity. It does not involve the sharing of commissions. Nor does the income received by regional firms in executing orders in multiple listings depend upon the willingness of national brokerage firms to reciprocate. The possibility of monopolistic practices is thus reduced. As a further point, multiple trading facilitates reciprocation by augmenting the number of issues in which it is permitted.

The amount of multiple trading warranted on this basis is difficult to determine. For those brokerage firms which are members of both the national and regional exchanges, the presumption is that regional trading in national listings is avoided except where matters of reciprocity are involved. The avowed reason is that the accounting procedures of national firms are designed to handle the transmission of orders to the national exchanges more efficiently than to the regional exchanges. For regional brokerage firms, orders to buy or sell nationally listed issues are forwarded to regional exchanges wherever possible and may well exceed those in regional issues.

Whatever the conclusions reached as to the appropriate volume of regional trading in national listings, lasting strength on the part of regional exchanges presupposes a substantial base of regional listings. Ratios of transactions in multiply traded issues to aggregate activity on regional exchanges provide information of this kind and reveal the current emphasis of regional exchanges.

RELIANCE UPON MULTIPLE TRADING BY REGIONAL EXCHANGES

Table 2 shows the relationship of share volume in multiply traded issues to total volume for seven leading regional exchanges during the years 1944, 1948, 1952, and 1953. The aggregate ratio for these exchanges exceeds 50 per cent in each of the four years and appears to be increasing through time.[2] Only in the cases of the Los Angeles and San Francisco stock exchanges are the individual ratios substantially below 50 per cent.

As used in table 2, the term "multiply traded issues" refers only

---

[2] For prewar data and further confirmation of this statement, see J. O. Kamm, *The Decentralization of Securities Exchanges* (Boston: Meador Publishing Co., 1942), p. 124.

to those issues which are listed on the New York Stock Exchange and are available for trading on one or more of the seven largest regional exchanges. Multiple trading also arises in connection with stocks listed on the American Exchange, but is of relatively little consequence in the aggregative sense. Expressed as a percentage of total physical transactions, trading in American listings approximated 3 and 6 per cent in 1954 for the San Francisco and Los Angeles exchanges.

In individual cases, the degree of market splitting occasioned by multiple trading is likely to be more important for the American Exchange than for the New York Exchange. The reason is simply that the American Exchange represents the first gradation

TABLE 3

RATIOS OF ANNUAL TRADING IN 1954 ON THE SAN FRANCISCO AND LOS ANGELES EXCHANGES TO TOTAL SHARES OUTSTANDING FOR 40 ISSUES DUALLY TRADED ON THE AMERICAN EXCHANGE

Companies	(1) Shares outstanding	(2) 1954 transactions		Ratio of 2 to 1	
		Los Angeles exch.	San Francisco exch.	Los Angeles issues (per cent)	San Francisco issues (per cent)
Allied Artist Picture Corp.	869,185	6,676	......	1	...
Bailey Selburn Oil & Gas	2,429,669	......	870	...	a
Baldwin Securities Corp.	2,341,721	1,167	1,624	a	a
Beckman Instrument Co., Inc.	1,249,735	7,552	3,992	1	a
Bunker Hill and Sullivan Mining & Concent'g Co.	1,308,000	......	15,259	...	1
C and C Sugar Corp.	7,876,377	1,429	......	a	...
Calamba Sugar Estate Inc.	250,000	......	9,717	...	4
Canada Southern Petroleum Ltd.[b]	4,982,952	2,116	......	a	...
Canadian Atlantic Oil Co., Ltd.	3,181,671	64,066	88,917	2	3
Canadian Homestead Oils Ltd.	924,753	1,450	187	a	e
Canso Natural Gas, Ltd., Voting[b]	3,114,315	2,285	......	a	...
Canso Oil Producers, Ltd., Voting	2,491,476	557	......	a	...
Cenco Corp.	980,956	6,631	......	1	...
Cessna Aircraft Co.	731,109	4,531	......	1	...
Charter Oil Co., Ltd.	2,322,852	40,415	......	2	...
Consolidated Engin. Corp.	890,459	29,469	......	3	...
Consolidated Liquidating Corp.	c	4,257	......	...	...
Electrodata Corp.	700,000	52,035	......	7	...
Emsco Mfg. Co.	457,786	0,129	......	a	...
Federated Petroleums, Ltd.	3,658,144	......	7,258	...	a
Fitzsimmons Stores, Ltd.	522,082	72,264	......	14	...
Gladding McBean and Co.	525,000	25,414	11,751	5	2

TABLE 3 (*Continued*)

Companies	(1) Shares outstanding	(2) 1954 transactions		Ratio of 2 to 1	
		Los Angeles exch.	San Francisco exch.	Los Angeles issues (per cent)	San Francisco issues (per cent)
Great Lakes Oil and Chemical Company...................	2,998,960	240,209	......	8	...
Kropp Forge Co..................	1,209,999	2,233	......	a	...
Le Tourneau (R. G.), Inc..........	503,370	......	......	...	...
New Idria Mining and Chemical Co. .	2,588,962	46,032	......	2	...
New Park Mining Co..............	3,056,228	......	3,035	a	...
Oceanic Oil Co..................	1,796,653	293,380	258,053	16	14
Oliver United Filters Inc. (class B)...	198,891	......	18,049	...	9
Pacific Can Co. c................	420,000	......	7,781	...	2
Pioneer Gold Mines of B. C., Ltd.....	1,751,750	......	......	...	...
Puget Sound Pulp and Timber Company....................	778,171	1,018	11,256	a	1
Rome Cable Corp................	513,416	0,167	......	a	...
Ryan Aeronautical Co.............	434,093	38,025	380	9	a
Sapphire Petroleum Ltd.d.........	5,727,511	43,123	......	1	...
Superior Portland Cement Inc.......	271,700	......	345	...	a
Tishman Realty and Construction Co...........................	400,000	......	......	...	...
Trans-Empire Oils, Ltd............	2,417,750	406	......	a	...
Universal Consolidated Oil Co.......	639,410	17,400	2,326	3	a
Utah Idaho Sugar Co..............	2,371,283	......	9,541	...	a
Total e......................	1,004,236	450,341			

SOURCE: Annual *Summaries of Transactions* for the San Francisco and Los Angeles Exchanges.
a Less than 1 per cent.
b On April 20, 1954, Canada Southern Oil split into Canso Oil, Canso Natural Gas, and Canada Southern Petroleum (all shares held in a voting trust).
c Recently acquired by National Can Company. There will be no further reports in Standard and Poor's.
d Before May 31, 1954, shares outstanding were 4,820,976. On that date, shares were increased to 6,378,465. A weighted average of these is employed.
e

$$\frac{\text{LA partial total}}{\text{all trans.}} \quad \frac{1,004,236}{17,791,645} = .056.$$

$$\frac{\text{SF partial total}}{\text{all trans.}} \quad \frac{450,341}{16,302,149} = .027.$$

beyond regional exchanges, and many issues listed thereon still possess strong regional characteristics. To demonstrate this point, 1954 ratios of annual trading to shares outstanding are derived for San Francisco and Los Angeles listings which are dually traded on the American Exchange and exhibited in table 3. In 14 of 40 instances, the 1954 turnover ratios equal 2 per cent or more; in 8

instances, they equal or exceed 5 per cent. The significance of
regional trading in these issues becomes apparent when it is observed that the aggregate annual turnover of shares traded on the
American Exchange averaged 15 per cent for the period 1950–
1954.[3]

If multiple-trading ratios were redesigned to contrast dollar,
rather than physical, magnitudes, the results would presumably
reveal even greater reliance by most regional exchanges upon multiple listings. The point is that the average market price of stocks
listed on the New York Stock Exchange is almost universally higher
than that of primary regional listings. Sample surveys of the San
Francisco Exchange for three different trading days show striking
disparities between ratios based on share and dollar volume.[4] In
terms of share volume, multiple-trading ratios for the three days
range between 40 and 50 per cent, whereas in terms of dollar
volume they range between 80 and 90 per cent.

BENEFITS DERIVED FROM MULTIPLE TRADING

One argument for regional trading in national listings has already
been presented. Before admitting the percentage of trading in multiple listings as evidence, consideration should be given to the possibility that multiple trading can be justified on other grounds as
well.

Multiple trading affords at least three conceivable advantages.[5]
Total trading in national listings may be augmented by the selling
endeavor of regional members which are not associated with the
New York exchanges. The location of regional exchanges in different time zones throughout the United States lengthens the trading day for multiply listed issues. Finally, the presence of several
specialists, as opposed to one or a very few, may contribute to the
market stability of multiple listings.

Specific note is made of the effect of multiple trading upon the
aggregate activity of nationally listed stocks by Ronald E. Kaehler,
president of the San Francisco Exchange, in a prepared statement
before the Senate Committee on Banking and Currency. In his
testimony, Mr. Kaehler states:[6]

---

[3] See table 7.

[4] The dates, chosen at random, are October 14, 1954, December 7, 1954, and March
22, 1955.

[5] The good-will argument which is often utilized by regional exchanges to induce
national firms to list their securities regionally is ignored. The important consideration is the actual trading which may also be done under "unlisted trading privileges."

[6] *Stock Market Study Hearings*, 84th Cong., 1st sess. (Washington, 1955), p. 241.

The governing board and members of the San Francisco Stock Exchange are firmly convinced that trading in "dual" issues by our exchange does not constitute a duplication of trading on the New York Stock Exchange, but on the contrary provides an important supplementary market which has proven to be in the public interest. Members of our

TABLE 4

RATIOS OF ANNUAL TRADING ON THE SAN FRANCISCO EXCHANGE TO TOTAL SHARES OUTSTANDING FOR 14 CALIFORNIA COMPANIES WITH NATIONAL LISTINGS DURING THE PERIOD 1949–1955

Stock	1954	1953	1952	1951	1950	1949
Pabco Products	6.9	6.5	7.0	5.6	9.9	...
Rheem Mfg.	4.4	3.7	5.1	5.2	5.4	1.9
P. G. & E.	2.2	2.4	3.1	3.8	5.4	3.3
Safeway Stores	1.7	2.1	1.7	1.0	1.3	0.9
Calif. Packing	3.8	1.9	1.6	1.2	4.3	2.2
Transamerica	2.1	1.8	3.2	3.9	5.7	4.8
Lockheed Aircraft	2.9	1.6	1.2	0.8	2.3	1.5
So. Calif. Edison	1.4	1.5	1.0	0.8	1.2	1.5
Kaiser A.C.—Pfd.	2.5	1.4	1.1	...	...	...
Crown Zellerbach	0.86	1.2	1.1	1.6	3.3	3.2
So. Pacific Co.	1.6	0.9	0.3	1.0	1.6	1.3
Food Machinery	0.9	0.6	0.8	1.0	0.9	0.7
Caterpillar Tractor	0.8	0.8	0.7	0.7	1.2	0.6
Std. Oil of Calif.	0.7	0.6	0.6	0.6	1.2	0.8
Kaiser A. C.—Com.	0.8	0.5	0.7	0.7	...	...
Richfield	0.4	0.3	0.4	0.4	0.8	1.9

SOURCE: *Annual Summary of Transactions,* 1949–1955, San Francisco Stock Exchange.

exchange generate orders in these securities for the very reason that they are traded here. If they were not listed locally, member firms might well recommend to their clients other securities of equal value that were listed locally rather than those traded only in eastern markets.

Evidence to support this contention is provided by Carl E. Ogren, vice-president and secretary of the Midwest Exchange. Mr. Ogren comments in correspondence that:

Many companies originally listed in the east have listed on this exchange for the primary purpose of attracting a broader stockholder interest in this area and to make available profitable dealings in their issues by the 180 member firms of this Exchange who are not members of the eastern exchanges.

These 180 brokerage firms constitute, it should be observed, almost two-thirds of all member firms of the Midwest Exchange.

Of special relevance, as far as the influence upon total transactions is concerned, is regional trading in the issues of nationally known corporations whose principal office or activity is in the area serviced by a given regional exchange. For reasons of association with a particular locale, listing on the appropriate regional exchange may stimulate additional interest in the stocks of these companies. To test this point, ratios of annual trading on the San Francisco Exchange to total shares outstanding for 16 California firms whose securities are listed nationally are shown in table 4 for the years 1949 to 1955. Although it cannot be demonstrated conclusively that total volume is in fact increased through regional trading, these turnover ratios are sufficiently large in several instances to suggest that such may be the case.

Elongated trading periods enable investors on the East Coast to buy or sell multiply traded issues until late afternoon and permit West Coast trading to be carried on during the normal business day. In accordance with time differentials, the Los Angeles and San Francisco stock exchanges terminate trading two hours subsequent to the New York exchanges. Although the New York exchanges could eliminate this advantage by closing later, it is conceivable that the post-closing volume can be handled more efficiently by the regional exchanges.[7]

In order to test the significance of this factor, a sample of 18 multiply listed issues traded on both the New York and San Francisco exchanges is selected. For each of these stocks, morning (7:00–12:30) trading on the San Francisco Stock Exchange is contrasted with afternoon (12:30–2:30) activity during November, 1954. The results of this comparison are shown in table 5.

If the benefits derived from lengthened trading are significant, afternoon activity in multiple listings should be relatively heavy. Ratios of afternoon trading to total volume in joint listings ought therefore to exceed the ratio of afternoon hours to the total trading day, which approximates 27 per cent for the San Francisco Exchange.

Following this line of reasoning, the relationships shown in table 5 for the sample issues deny the existence of important advantages from longer trading days. For the 18 issues as a whole, the after-

---

[7] Interestingly enough, however, the West Coast exchanges appear to rely less upon multiple trading than any of the other leading regional exchanges.

TABLE 5

RATIOS OF AFTERNOON TRADING TO TOTAL TRANSACTIONS ON THE SAN FRANCISCO
EXCHANGE IN 18 ISSUES TRADED JOINTLY ON THE NEW YORK AND
SAN FRANCISCO EXCHANGE

(Arranged by issue and by day, for November, 1954, in per cent)

Issue	Ratio of afternoon to total trading	Date (Nov. 1954)	Ratio of afternoon to total trading —18 issues
Allis Chalmers	.....	1	11.90
American Airlines	6.52	3	6.49
American Telephone and Telegraph	.....	4	3.13
		5	5.17
California Packing	21.67	8	5.36
Celanese	2.78	9	7.50
Commonwealth Edison	.....	10	4.65
		11	5.13
		12	23.19
General Motors	15.79	15	7.04
International Harvester	4.23	16	18.64
		17	5.88
Pacific Gas and Electric	4.55	18	9.52
		19	2.27
Radio Corporation of America	.....	22	14.55
		23	5.88
Republic Steel	5.88	24	3.33
Rheem	7.89	26	10.00
Sperry	4.00	29	6.00
Tidewater	9.87	30	.....
Transamerica	11.06		
Greyhound	8.70		
International Tel. and Tel.	7.32		
Union Oil	9.09		

SOURCE: Records of the San Francisco Stock Exchange.

noon-to-total-volume ratio approaches 27 per cent only twice during the entire month. The highest ratio throughout the period for any single security is about 22 per cent.

From time to time, unusual activity in multiple listings occurs during afternoon sessions on the San Francisco Exchange. On January 25, 1955, when the directors of United States Steel raised common dividends and proposed a stock split, some 9,400 shares were traded after 12:30. On February 8, 1955, when the directors of Western Union raised common dividends and proposed a stock split, some 2,700 shares were traded after the closing of the New York Stock Exchange. Cases of this type do not arise with sufficient frequency for our conclusions to be amended.

The influence of multiple listing upon the number of specialists responsible for each stock is potentially the most significant aspect of multiple trading. At least one specialist is assigned to every stock traded on each exchange.[8] As indicated previously, specialists not only match orders to buy against orders to sell, but also stabilize prices and augment market continuity by taking positions.

The more specialists interested in a given stock, the greater are likely to be the resources available to carry out the market stabilization function. Combined round-lot, odd-lot arrangements by the leading regional exchanges contribute additional financial strength to the specialist group. In the Los Angeles Exchange which inaugurated the combined system as recently as August, 1954, for example, provision was made for fourteen specialist odd-lot dealers, each assigned to some 26 separate stocks.[9]

Although multiple listing augments the number of specialists, a counter argument which hinges upon the splintering of the securities market merits attention. To the extent that multiple listing reduces the volume of transactions in individual stocks traded on the New York exchanges, specialists on these exchanges must be assigned a larger number of issues to offset the diminished volume. The consequence is that less attention and less resources are likely to be devoted to multiply traded securities by specialists on the national exchanges than would otherwise be the case. A further point is that regional specialists may be unwilling to accept much, if any, responsibility for stabilizing the market for national listings.[10]

Arbitrage operations mitigate, but do not eliminate, the influence of the splintering effect. By arbitrage is meant that wherever multiple trading exists, divergent price movements for individual stocks tend to be counteracted by the placing of simultaneous orders to buy on one exchange and to sell on the other.

Accelerated transfers of stock, another possible advantage of multiple listing, has significance principally in connection with the

[8] An exception, which is of no relevance to the present discussion, is that inactive issues may be traded on a negotiated basis with no specialist assigned to them.

[9] "Los Angeles Stock Exchange Starts New Odd Lot System," *Wall Street Journal* (Pacific Coast edition, July 22, 1954).

[10] It is nonetheless interesting to observe that regional specialists are often more willing to assume positions in multiply traded issues (because of their relatively high liquidity) than in regional listings over which they have exclusive jurisdiction.

declaration of dividends and rights. The speed of transfer determines the period of ex-rights and ex-dividends.

So far as the San Francisco Exchange is representative of regional exchanges in general, this point is of little consequence. The San Francisco Exchange is concerned primarily with matching, rather than surpassing, the transfer period set by the New York Stock Exchange. Some diversity may occur in the *cash* trading dates. These differences are attributable to the required shipment time and ordinarily appear to favor the New York Stock Exchange.

Granted that the existence of regional exchanges is justifiable, independently of multiple listings, regional trading in issues listed on the national exchanges may well permit more efficient procedures on the part of regional exchanges. Necessary conditions for this result to obtain are the presence of relatively heavy fixed costs and of economies of scale. From an over-all point of view, the gains to regional exchanges from multiple trading should exceed the losses to the national exchanges. Whether such is likely to be the case is examined subsequently in connection with our review of merger possibilities for regional exchanges.

Multiple trading may of course increase the total volume of transactions on regional exchanges by less than the amount of regional trading in national listings. To the extent that members of regional exchanges devote attention to multiple listings, interest in regional listings is likely to decline below what it otherwise would be. Despite this consideration, two factors suggest that the existence of multiply traded issues contributes to aggregate activity on regional exchanges. One is that selling effort per transaction unit is relatively low for nationally known issues. A given amount of effort allocated between regional and multiple listings will therefore produce a larger volume of transactions than an equivalent amount directed solely to the sale of regional issues. The other and related item is that multiply traded offerings enable member firms of regional exchanges to obtain and hold customers which might otherwise deal only with members of the New York Stock Exchange.

As a final point, it should be observed that odd-lot volume on regional exchanges is proportionately greater for multiple listings than is round-lot volume. Evidence of this is to be found in table 6 in which round- and odd-lot trading in dual listings is compared for the New York and Midwest stock exchanges. To the extent that odd-lot transactions in multiply traded issues predominate on regional exchanges, arguments relating to market splintering lose force. Odd-lot dealers operate independently of specialists on the New York Stock Exchange. Their effect upon round-lot volume is thus uncertain and is dependent upon their inability to pair off odd-lot purchases against odd-lot sales.[11]

Interestingly enough, the execution of odd-lot orders on regional exchanges may actually augment round-lot trading on the New

TABLE 6

RELATION BETWEEN STOCK VOLUME IN DUAL LISTINGS ON THE NEW YORK AND MIDWEST STOCK EXCHANGES FOR THE PERIOD 1944–1955
(in per cent)

Year	Odd-lot volume	Round-lot volume	Combined volume
1944	11.4	4.8	6.2
1945	11.6	4.2	5.8
1946	8.3	3.1	4.3
1947	8.5	2.5	3.7
1948	8.8	2.7	3.9
1949	10.7	3.1	4.5
1950	11.5	3.9	5.1
1951	12.3	3.9	5.3
1952	11.9	4.2	5.6
1953	11.6	3.8	5.2
1954[a]	10.5	3.6	4.7
Average	10.6	3.6	4.9

SOURCE: Department of Research and Statistics, New York Stock Exchange.
[a] First six months.

York Stock Exchange in some cases. According to one study, one-third of the odd-lot business transacted in multiply traded issues on the Boston Exchange during early 1940 ultimately reached the New York Exchange in the form of round-lot orders.[12] For the same period, less than one-sixth of the odd-lot trading on the New York Exchange was reflected in round-lot transactions.

The preceding justifications for multiple trading appear to possess restricted significance at best. Although some regional trading in national listings can perhaps be condoned, primary dependence

[11] That is to say, odd-lot dealers adjust their positions to desired levels through the placement of orders to buy or sell round-lots with the specialists.

[12] Kamm, *op. cit.*, p. 63.

by regional exchanges upon multiply traded securities cannot be sanctioned. Multiple-trading ratios are thus accepted as a partial indication of the caliber of regional exchanges.

CONCLUSIONS CONCERNING MULTIPLE TRADING

The level of multiple-trading ratios, shown in table 2, suggests that regional exchanges are primarily concerned with their status as independent branches of the national exchanges. The implication

TABLE 7

ANNUAL TURNOVER OF OUTSTANDING SHARES FOR THE NEW YORK
AND AMERICAN STOCK EXCHANGES

Year	Ratio of yearly transactions to total shares outstanding	
	New York Stock Exchange[a]	American Stock Exchange
1950...	23	18
1951...	18	16
1952...	13	14
1953...	12	12
Unweighted average.........................	17	15

SOURCE: New York Stock Exchange, *Year Book*, 1954, p. 34; American Stock Exchange, Division of Research.
[a] Listed shares.

is that regional exchanges have been unsuccessful in holding regional issues and in acquiring new regional listings. Whether the current emphasis is attributable to the attitudes of exchange members, to deficiencies in the procedures of regional exchanges, or to other factors cannot be ascertained from multiple-trading ratios alone.

In the event the New York exchanges decide to allow discounts on commission charges to nonmember firms, regional exchanges are likely to experience significant reductions in transactions volume. The case for reciprocity then diminishes, if not disappears. Although the attrition may be gradual, other bases for regional trading in national listings lack force.

Examination of multiple-trading ratios reveals that the California exchanges possess the most substantial assortment of regional listings. From this point of view, they appear to be the most effective of all regional exchanges.

COMPARISON WITH NEW YORK EXCHANGES

Both the preëminence of the New York exchanges and the fact that regional exchanges are closely patterned after them suggest the possibility of utilizing the national exchanges as a further basis for evaluating regional security exchanges. Relationships, such as turnover of outstanding shares and average daily trading per issue, provide at least in part the requisite tools for a comparative analysis of this type. If not comprehensive, some insight should at a minimum be gained into the nature and relative status of regional exchanges.

Whenever relative standards are employed, two fundamental questions arise. One relates to whether the measure used is ideal in any realistic sense of the word. The other pertains to whether the standard employed is appropriate.

Utilization of the New York exchanges as guides to the effectiveness of regional exchanges falls short of perfection on both counts. Although successfully operated, the national exchanges themselves admit the need for improvement.[13] Because of their relatively greater prestige and relatively smaller contact with over-the-counter markets, moreover, the national exchanges qualify only as "limited" standards for judging regional exchanges. In view of these deficiencies and restrictions imposed by available data, attention is directed for the most part at general, rather than detailed, comparisons.

MARKETABILITY AS EVIDENCED BY TRADING VOLUME

Of fundamental importance, when contrasting subdivisions of the securities market, is trading volume. The level of trading activity determines in large part the ability of any given segment of the securities market to absorb orders to buy or sell securities without undue fluctuations in prices or other disruption. For comparative purposes, transactions volume must be expressed in terms of individual issues and of appropriate time periods and must be related to the number of shares outstanding.

In the organized exchanges the proper unit of time appears to be the *trading day*. Orders at market are forwarded to the floor of the exchange for immediate execution. Although limited orders

---

[13] In the 1952 *Annual Report* of the New York Stock Exchange, p. 10, for example, reference is made to a study of operations and functions, initiated "because of the apparent inability of the Exchange to make the maximum effective contribution to the growth of the economy."

away from market may be carried over from one day to the next, their execution depends upon the flow of market orders.

When transactions volume is expressed in terms of average daily trading per issue, significant differences can be observed among organized exchanges. The average of daily trading in each issue during 1953 amounts to slightly more than 900 shares for the New York Stock Exchange, as contrasted with 548 shares for the American Stock Exchange. Corresponding figures for the San Francisco, Midwest, and Los Angeles exchanges are 178, 151, and 121 shares respectively. Absolute levels of average daily volume per issue vary from period to period in accordance with changes in the state of expectations in the securities market, but the relative position of each exchange remains much the same.

Before accepting the differential in average daily trading per issue as evidence that the marketability of issues traded on the national exchanges is generally superior to that of shares traded on regional exchanges, consideration should be given to the impact of concentrations in security holdings.[14] Concentrated holdings exert opposing influences upon marketability. So far as large blocks are characterized by inactivity, the magnitude of day-to-day fluctuations in the prices of stocks thus affected may be relatively small under ordinary circumstances. Under extraordinary conditions, however, marketability may be seriously impaired thereby. Efforts to dispose of large holdings in the face of restricted activity impose a severe strain upon organized exchanges and encourage the use of over-the-counter channels.

For issues listed on the national exchanges, institutional investments present the most difficulty. Institutional investments, including those of bank-administered personal trusts, in equity shares listed on the New York Stock Exchange amounted to approximately $40,000,000,000 as of the end of 1953.[15] The National Association of Security Dealers estimates, based upon a sampling of "typical" cases, that the annual portfolio turnover for discretionary bank common trusts is in the neighborhood of 5 per cent and that turnover for insurance companies is noticeably lower.[16] Sales of securities by open-end investment companies, in contrast, amounted to 15 per cent of net assets during 1954.

---

[14] As used in this context, marketability refers to the perfection of the markets in which assets are bought and sold. That is to say, it pertains to the ability of holders to convert securities into cash without seriously affecting their price.

[15] New York Stock Exchange, *Annual Report*, 1953, p. 6.

[16] *Stock Market Study Hearings*, 84th Cong., 1st sess. (Washington, 1955), p. 355.

As indicated by the low turnover of their holdings, institutions—with the possible exception of investment companies—are less inclined than individuals to trade actively. It may be concluded that heavy investment by institutions in equity shares adversely affects exchange activity. Whenever portfolio readjustments are sought, moreover, single transactions are likely to be relatively large in relation to average daily trading per issue on the New York exchanges. Because of their size, institutional orders to buy and sell shares cannot readily be absorbed by auction-type markets as presently constituted, and are frequently channeled through the over-the-counter markets.

Although untroubled by institutional holdings, regional exchanges are confronted with an analogous problem. The characteristics of regional corporations, together with less stringent criteria for listing issues on regional exchanges than on the national exchanges, imply the likelihood of considerable concentrations in shareholdings.[17] So far as the primary objective behind such holdings is perpetuation of control, their effect is to thin, but not necessarily disrupt, the market. In the event that sizable blocks of regionally listed issues become available for distribution, regional exchanges can provide marketability only indirectly through their influence upon negotiated prices.

Our conclusion is that, so far as it exists, the concentrated ownership of listed shares circumscribes their marketability. Since both national and regional exchanges have to contend with this problem, albeit for different reasons, the utilization of average daily trading per issue as a measure of relative marketability continues to be valid.

Other indicators of trading activity exist. Perhaps the most common of these is share turnover, which relates the physical volume of transactions to total shares outstanding. Since it is expressed in ratio form, the use of share turnover facilitates comparisons among organized exchanges whose size differential is substantial. Equality of share turnover figures for national and regional exchanges suggests that regional exchanges provide markets for their listings comparable to those furnished by national exchanges when the

---

[17] As suggested previously, the stringency of criteria for listing appears to vary directly with the size and position of the exchange. The New York Stock Exchange prescribes that at least 300,000 shares must be outstanding, exclusive of concentrated ownerships, and that holders, discounting odd-lot commitments, must number 1,500. The San Francisco Stock Exchange, in contrast, sets up no definite criteria except that 20 per cent of the shares outstanding should be publicly owned.

TABLE 8

ANNUAL TURNOVER OF OUTSTANDING SHARES FOR 25 SAN FRANCISCO LISTINGS DURING
THE YEARS 1949–1955
(Ranked according to 1953 data)

	1954	1953	1952	1951	1950	1949	Average
Golden State........	....	43.1	14.4	19.9	20.8	13.6	22.36
M J M and M......	19.8	39.3	36.4	64.9	26.9	5.7	32.17
Atok-B.W.........	5.1	35.9	10.3	5.3	1.4	0.8	9.80
Dominguez........	17.2	21.1	13.3	10.1	11.5	11.9	14.18
Id-Md............	22.4	20.8	18.2	14.7	11.2	13.7	16.83
El Dorado........	49.2	19.1	24.6	14.9	19.2	10.2	22.87
Palmer Stendel.....	19.3	17.6	....	....	....	....	18.45
General Paint......	19.6	17.5	16.5	14.5	17.6	9.6	15.88
S and W FF........	18.1	16.4	22.5	12.7	7.9	6.0	13.93
Blair Holdings......	35.9	13.7	12.8	13.6	13.4	15.1	17.42
Oceanic Oil.........	14.3	12.2	25.3	8.0	7.8	3.8	9.75
Westates Pfd.......	25.1	11.8	13.2	16.3	16.8	18.2	16.90
Pac Coast Agg......	16.8	10.7	11.2	15.8	16.4	10.8	13.62
Central Eureka.....	15.8	9.6	13.7	25.6	29.1	34.7	21.41
Calaveras.........	18.3	9.6	8.6	16.4	30.8	47.9	21.93
Westates Com......	23.7	8.9	11.0	13.6	15.2	31.8	17.37
Marchant.........	20.1	7.7	3.0	12.7	13.9	8.4	10.97
Intex Oil..........	5.3	6.4	19.2	12.9	8.9	16.2	11.48
Anglo Calif........	4.5	6.1	9.0	9.4	8.6	8.1	7.62
Emp.-Capwell......	9.9	5.9	5.9	7.4	9.2	8.3	7.77
Hawaiian Pineapple.	6.0	5.7	8.2	4.8	3.7	2.4	5.13
Matson............	5.7	4.5	4.0	3.9	5.3	4.5	4.66
West Dept Stores...	8.9	4.5	6.8	4.7	15.7	6.7	7.88
Menasco..........	4.9	3.9	2.9	5.0	10.7	3.3	5.12
Morr-Knudsen.....	....	3.1	2.8	2.4	4.7	6.0	3.80

SOURCE: San Francisco Stock Exchange, *Summary of Transactions*, 1949–1955.

nature of the issue is considered. Variations in marketability can, under these circumstances, be attributed to differences in the size of issues traded on the various exchanges. Deviations of share turnovers for regional exchanges from those for national exchanges indicate better or worse performance.

Annual share turnover data for the New York and American stock exchanges are shown in table 7, covering the years 1950 to 1953 inclusive. The turnover of shares on both exchanges is surprisingly similar. Their combined, unweighted annual average for the four-year period approximates 16 per cent. Interestingly enough, the trend in share turnover has been downward in the past several decades, reflecting either poorer performance on the part of the national exchanges or changes in the structure of the securities market and in the nature of security holders. The latter is probably the most important influence.

To facilitate comparisons of turnover ratios with the New York exchanges, a sample of 25 issues, traded primarily on the San Francisco Stock Exchange, is chosen. The basis for selection is trading activity during 1953. With the exception of multiply traded issues and issues whose price per share is below $1, these 25 issues represent the volume leaders for the San Francisco Exchange. Since the proportion of relatively inactive stocks appears to be greater for the San Francisco Exchange than for the New York exchanges, the utilization of a sample is deemed realistic.

Ratios of annual transactions to shares outstanding for each of the 25 issues are shown in table 8, encompassing the period 1949 to 1955. The diversity of results exhibited therein clearly circumscribes the meaningfulness of averages.[18] It can nevertheless be observed that the median turnover for these stocks lies below the aggregate figures for the New York exchanges in each of the four years for which comparisons are available. Median turnover ratios approximate 11 for 1950, 13 for 1951, 12 for 1952, and 10 for 1953. These median ratios, it may also be noted, exceed the unweighted averages of annual turnovers for *all* regional San Francisco listings, which approximated 9 per cent for 1954. Our conclusion is that the San Francisco Exchange is distinctly inferior to the national exchanges in this respect.

In view of its size and of its relatively small interest in multiple trading, the performance of the San Francisco Exchange is presumed to equal or exceed that of any other regional exchange in the United States. If Canadian exchanges are regarded as regional exchanges for the sake of comparison, however, the performance of even the New York exchanges may be surpassed. By way of illustration, the aggregate annual turnover ratios for the Toronto Stock Exchange were 18 for 1953 and 21 for 1954.[19]

Closely associated with the question of over-all trading activity

---

[18] The high level exhibited by at least two of the turnover ratios is, moreover, directly attributable to merger activity. Both El Dorado and Golden State have recently been acquired by Foremost Dairies.

[19] Toronto Stock Exchange, *Monthly Review*, December, 1953, and December, 1954.

is that of whether or not issues traded on the various security exchanges possess reasonably uniform marketability. Although prominent stocks feature exceptional trading activity with good cause, successful exchanges require, as a rule, substantial numbers of active issues. Otherwise, elaborate trading procedures cannot easily be justified. Nor can the exchange be said to have a solid foundation.

Perhaps the best measure of uniform marketability, or absence thereof, is trading concentration. A high degree of concentration in physical volume of trading among a few issues may result from one or more factors. It may reflect—and this is subject to verification—the presence of low-priced stocks which encourage speculative activity and exhibit relatively violent fluctuations in prices. When expressed in terms of dollar value, however, transactions in low-priced issues need not represent an unduly large proportion of aggregate activity. The principal danger of low-priced stocks is that the behavior of such issues will adversely influence that of other listings.

A high degree of concentration may be attributable to inadequacies in selection processes, listing requirements, and removal criteria. It may also be the consequence of trading procedures which are not effectively designed to promote activity in a wide variety of issues. Both of these considerations are believed to be important and are treated elsewhere.

The implications of undue concentration, when associated with regional exchanges, are analogous in at least one respect to those of multiple trading. Each raises questions concerning both the economic justification of regional exchanges as presently constituted and the desirability of mergers among regional exchanges. Unless factors contributing to excessive concentration can be counteracted, strong arguments exist for either eliminating the exchanges in question and transferring the active issues to the national exchanges or consolidating 2 or more of these exchanges.

Ratios of transactions in leading issues to total trading are shown in table 9 for both the national exchanges and the San Francisco, Midwest, and Los Angeles exchanges. As might be anticipated, substantial concentration in trading occurs at all levels. Approximately 3.3 per cent of the issues traded on the New York Stock Exchange accounts for almost one-fourth of total transactions during 1952 and 1953. Approximately 6.2 per cent of the stocks traded on the American Stock Exchange accounts for about one-half of aggregate activity during the same period.

In a similar fashion, 5.1 per cent of the issues traded on the San

Francisco Exchange provides nearly one-half of total physical volume during 1954. The existence of low-priced stocks, it may be observed, noticeably affects the results. Transactions volume in six listings whose average prices range from $.035 to $1.45 constitutes roughly 29 per cent of total activity during 1954.[20]

The situation in the Los Angeles Exchange is not far different. Approximately 7.7 per cent of the stocks traded contributes almost

TABLE 9

RATIOS TO TOTAL VOLUME OF TRADING IN THE MOST ACTIVE ISSUES TRADED ON THE NEW YORK STOCK EXCHANGE, THE AMERICAN STOCK EXCHANGE, AND SELECTED REGIONAL EXCHANGES

Exchange and year	Ratio to total volume of trading			
	First 20 issues	First 30 issues	First 40 issues	First 50 issues
New York				
1952.................	.....	17.40	21.05	24.35
1953.................	.....	16.96	20.99	24.55
American				
1952.................	.....	40.56	47.12	52.46
1953.................	.....	35.79	41.80	46.81
San Francisco				
1954.................	47.23	52.84	.....	.....
Los Angeles				
1954.................	39.50	46.76	.....	.....
Midwest				
1954.................	17.60[a]	23.85[a]	.....	.....

SOURCE: New York and American Stock exchanges, Department of Research and Statistics; Los Angeles, Midwest, and San Francisco exchanges, *Summaries of Transactions, 1954.*
[a] Ratio of round-lot only to total trading.

one-half of aggregate activity. The presence of low-priced issues again appreciably affects the degree of concentration. Nine issues whose average prices range from $.06 to $1.51 give rise to more than one-fourth of total trading in 1954.

Some 9 per cent of the stocks traded on the Midwest Exchange accounts for almost one-fourth of total transactions during 1954 on the basis of round-lots alone. The inclusion of odd-lot trading may well raise this proportion to one-third or more. As evidenced by the somewhat lower concentration ratios, low-priced shares exert less influence upon the Midwest Exchange than upon the San Francisco and Los Angeles exchanges.

[20] These prices are obtained by averaging the high and low prices for the period and, as such, are not true averages.

The fact that regional listings are not differentiated from multiply traded issues complicates interpretation of the preceding data. In order to test whether the concentration in trading for regional stocks diverges greatly from that for all issues, percentage distributions by volume classes are prepared for both regional and nationally listed issues traded on the San Francisco Exchange and are shown in table 10. Since 27 per cent of the regional stocks fall

TABLE 10

PERCENTAGE DISTRIBUTION BY VOLUME CLASSES OF REGIONAL AND NATIONALLY LISTED
ISSUES TRADED ON THE SAN FRANCISCO EXCHANGE (1954)

1954 share volume (ooo's)	National listings	Regional issues
100 and over................................	3	13
75–100.....................................	3	5
50–75......................................	7	9
25–50......................................	15	8
10–25......................................	27	17
Less than 10...............................	45	48
Total.....................................	100	100

SOURCE: San Francisco Stock Exchange, *Summary of Transactions,* 1954.

within the three top categories, as compared with 13 per cent for national listings, these distributions suggest that the degree of concentration may be somewhat greater for regional listings than for all issues traded on the San Francisco Exchange.[21]

From the material just presented, it cannot be concluded that the concentration in trading is greater for regional exchanges than for the New York exchanges. It can nevertheless be said that this factor is of more concern to regional exchanges than to the national exchanges. The reason is simply that regional exchanges possess lower trading bases.

To illustrate this point, let us assume that 5 per cent of the issues traded accounts for one-half of total volume on a given exchange, and that average daily trading per issue is 180 shares. Average daily trading for the top 5 per cent amounts to 342 shares, as contrasted with only 18 shares for the remainder. If the same concentration ratio obtains but average daily trading per issue is 900 shares, daily activity per issue for the top 5 per cent is 1,710 shares, as compared with 90 shares for the remainder.

---

[21] Note, however, the previous remarks pertaining to the relative importance of low-priced issues on regional exchanges.

The conclusion is that the national exchanges, by virtue of their relatively large average daily trading per issue, may still provide reasonably satisfactory markets for many of the less active stocks despite the observed concentration. This cannot, however, be said for the regional exchanges.

Each of the three measures thus far utilized suggest that the marketability of stocks traded on the New York exchanges is significantly better than that of issues traded primarily on regional exchanges. When multiple trading in national listings is considered, their marketability is further enhanced. Regional transactions in multiply traded issues amount to 7 or 8 per cent of their volume on the New York Stock Exchange.[22] In the case of General Motors, regional trading during 1953 approximated 22 per cent of the volume on the New York Stock Exchange.

DISTRIBUTION PROCEDURES

In part, the superior marketability which characterizes national listings is ascribable to the quality of the stock and the reputation of the issuer. In part, it is owing to the recognized status of the New York exchanges. The fact that a stock is listed on the national exchanges is often viewed as important both by the issuing company and by the investor. Whether the operating machinery of the New York exchanges functions more smoothly than that of regional exchanges is not immediately apparent. Because of its relevance to marketability, the matter of relative operating efficiency is now treated at some length.

The effective operation of organized exchanges requires both the rapid dissemination of information and the proper execution of what may be termed the economic function of speculation.[23] Unless price and volume data are immediately available, potential buyers and sellers of shares are unable to react quickly to price movements and thus to restore the market balance. Unless exchanges arrange to have temporary vacua in the flow of orders to buy or sell filled, short-term fluctuations in share prices may be excessive.

Prompt transmission of information facilitates arbitrage-like activities. As price relationships change for one reason or another,

---

[22] These data are furnished by G. Keith Funston, president of the New York Stock Exchange.

[23] By "economic function of speculation" is meant the stabilization of prices through time or, as applied to organized exchanges, the prevention of undue fluctuations in stock prices.

simultaneous orders to sell relatively overvalued stocks and to purchase relatively undervalued shares tend to restore the initial pattern. When believed to be of short duration, movements encompassing the market as a whole may also have their amplitude reduced through offsetting action of a similar type.

Both the New York exchanges and the leading regional exchanges utilize ticker systems to relay price and volume data to member firms. As evidenced by the following statistics, the national exchanges probably cover their trading areas more completely than do regional exchanges. At the beginning of 1955, the New York Stock Exchange had 2,186 stock tickers in operation in 384 cities.[24] As of the same date, the American Stock Exchange had 923 functioning tickers in 149 cities.[25] In addition, the New York and American stock exchanges had respectively 328 and 214 electrical quotation boards spread throughout the United States. The San Francisco Exchange, in contrast, had 25 tickers in operation at the end of 1954.

Since November 30, 1953, 3 leading regional exchanges have introduced systems which permit the transmittal, through floor microphones, of post quotations over private telephone wire with amplifiers placed at members' offices. The Midwest Exchange, with 57 members subscribing, initiated broadcasts on December 1, 1953.[26]

On July 20, 1954, the Los Angeles Exchange completed arrangements for its own program.[27] As in the Midwest Exchange, broadcasts originate from controlled microphones at the specialist quads and the ticker booth on the floor. Information of two types is disseminated in this fashion to subscribing members. Specialists pass along bids and offers in the hope of stimulating activity. Significant transactions and market flashes, as well as summaries of sales and quotes at established intervals, are also forwarded with the same purpose in mind. Present plans call for the ultimate extension of the broadcast circuit to outlying areas around Los Angeles.

In late 1954, the San Francisco Exchange put into operation similar facilities.[28] It, too, anticipates that trading activity will be augmented thereby.

[24] New York Stock Exchange, *Year Book,* 1955, p. 12.
[25] American Stock Exchange, *President's Report,* 1954–55, pp. 16–17.
[26] Midwest Stock Exchange, *Annual Report to Members,* November 30, 1953, p. 4.
[27] *Wall Street Journal,* July 16, 1954.
[28] It should perhaps to pointed out that information thus disseminated is not directly available to the investing public. Subscribing firms locate the loudspeakers in the offices of the trading departments, rather than on the main floors.

This method of dispersing information appears to possess excellent potential. As contrasted with ticker systems whose use is restricted to the public reporting of purchases and sales, broadcasting is susceptible of a variety of applications. Broadcasting permits incorporation of certain benefits of the negotiation-type market into the auction-type market. Although the coverage of broadcast systems is thus far limited, the circuits can readily be expanded if the experiment proves worthwhile. In this practice, therefore, the regional exchanges seem to have improved upon the procedures employed by the national exchanges.

However expeditious and comprehensive the dispersion of data, temporary disequilibria will at times occur in the supply-and-demand situation for individual issues. The spread between limited orders away from market may be excessive; and/or orders to buy (sell) may momentarily overwhelm orders to sell (buy). It is the function of *specialists* on both national and regional exchanges to mollify the impact upon stock prices of these short-lived phenomena.

Since specialists achieve market stabilization by assuming short or long positions as the occasion warrants, their chance for success depends upon both the availability of resources and the freedom with which they are allowed to operate. In recognition of these factors, the New York Stock Exchange, during 1953, doubled specialists' capital requirements and authorized "off the floor" purchases of blocks of listed securities by specialists and other parties under certain conditions. Floor trading rules were also liberalized during the same period.

It is reasonable to suppose that specialists on the New York exchanges are better able to preserve orderly markets than those on the regional exchanges. The superior activity which characterizes issues traded on the national exchanges enable specialists to concentrate upon relatively few stocks. The average number of issues assigned to each specialist by the New York and American Stock exchanges approximates 5 and 12 respectively, as compared with 26 by the Los Angeles Exchange and 29 by the San Francisco Exchange.[29]

The comparatively active trading in national listings benefits specialists on the New York exchanges in at least two ways. On the

---

[29] The utilization of averages is of course somewhat misleading. In the case of the American Stock Exchange, for example, the number of stocks in individual specialist books ranges from 3 to 60.

one hand, the task of the specialist is simplified. The wider the distribution of holdings and the larger the trading volume for any stock, the greater is the likelihood that the flow of orders to buy and to sell will be self-equating. To the extent that this is true, the need for specialists to take positions is correspondingly reduced. This condition does not of course prevail whenever the market is predominately bullish or bearish.

On the other hand, superior volume reflects greater willingness on the part of specialists to assume positions because of its relation to the depth of the specialist book. According to specialists on the San Francisco Exchange, the volume of limited orders awaiting execution is positively correlated with the level of activity in any given stock.[30] The flow of limited orders in turn affects the degree of risk associated with position-taking.

In order to elevate the specialists' position, regional exchanges combine the specialist and odd-lot functions under one person. The advantages of this amalgamation are twofold. Specialists can be assigned fewer issues than would otherwise be economically feasible.[31] They can also—in view of their odd-lot merchandising operations—be expected to assume larger positions if the occasion arises.

The relatively large number of issues assigned to specialists on regional exchanges poses fewer problems than might offhand be anticipated for yet another reason. As indicated previously, a substantial proportion of regionally traded stocks are listed on the national exchanges. For such issues regional specialists presumably assume only secondary responsibility for maintaining markets and can thus devote, if they so desire, more attention to securities which are not listed elsewhere.

Whether regional specialists are *willing*, despite their odd-lot functions, to devote much in the way of time and resources to assure the maintenance of satisfactory markets for regional issues is another matter. Conversations with the president of the San Francisco Exchange and with specialists thereon reveal that regional specialists are not disposed to assume substantial positions in regional issues. As a rule, specialists prefer neither to assume undue risks nor to tie up their funds for indefinite periods of time.

---

[30] Limited orders are defined as orders to buy or sell at specified prices. Market orders are defined as orders to buy or sell at the going market price.

[31] Note, however, that the combining of odd-lot and round-lot order execution increases specialist activity by less than the total of odd-lot trading. When the functions are separate, the odd-lot dealer buys and sells round-lots through the specialist.

Partial evidence of the comparative effectiveness of specialists on different exchanges in maintaining satisfactory markets is obtainable by reference to percentage spreads between bid and asked prices quoted by specialists. Average ratios of closing spreads to closing bid prices are shown in table 11 for *untraded* issues on the New York, American, San Francisco, and Los Angeles exchanges as of the approximate mid-points of five consecutive months. In deriving these averages, the individual ratios are assigned weights

TABLE 11

AVERAGE RATIOS OF SPREADS TO BID PRICES OF STOCK NOT TRADED FOR FOUR EXCHANGES

Date	New York Exchange	American Exchange	San Francisco Exchange	Los Angeles Exchange
1954				
October 12.................	2.04	4.34	8.37	3.36
November 12..............	2.44	2.82	5.16	5.87
December 14..............	2.61	3.40	4.39	2.57
1955				
January 12................	2.52	2.80	7.73	4.56
February 14...............	2.32	2.92	5.86	3.97
Average..............	2.39	3.26	6.30	4.07

SOURCE: *Wall Street Journal*, Pacific Coast edition.

according to stock prices in order to avoid undue distortion from low-priced issues. Since the willingness and ability of specialists to support less active stocks is of major interest, exclusive attention is devoted to untraded issues.

Relative spreads, as a rule, appear to vary inversely with the size of the organized exchange. For the dates examined, observed spreads for untraded stocks range from 2 to 2½ per cent of bid prices on the New York Stock Exchange, from approximately 3 to 4 per cent on the American Exchange, and from there on up on the regional exchanges. Since untraded issues on the Los Angeles Exchange average only 14 for the five days, little reliance is placed upon the average ratios for that exchange.

The utilization of simple, as opposed to weighted, averages of relative spreads accentuates the differential between the New York and American exchanges and between the national and regional exchanges. If simple averages are employed, ratios of spreads on untraded issues to bid prices approximate 9 per cent for the San

Francisco Exchange and 9½ per cent for the Los Angeles Exchange. The divergence between these relationships and those exhibited in table 11 reflect the negative correlation between relative spreads and stock prices. Since our primary concern is the comparative performance of specialists on different exchanges, however, the use of weighted averages of relative spreads is deemed preferable.

The data, shown in table 11, indicate that specialists on the national exchanges maintain closer markets for issues assigned to them than do regional specialists. Whether the performance of regional specialists is considered less satisfactory than that of specialists on the national exchanges in the light of the media traded depends upon judgment of the risks involved. The preceding remarks imply that regional specialists are not as effective as their national counterparts, but the case is not entirely clear.

If the New York exchanges function more smoothly than regional exchanges, it is primarily attributable to the tremendous size differential. The ability to specialize activities varies directly with total volume. Profit possibilities, and therefore the interest of exchange members in effective performance, exhibit a similar pattern. Funds for research, publicity, new facilities, and a variety of other uses are also more readily accessible to the national exchanges.

NEW LISTING POTENTIAL

Granted the importance of size, queries naturally arise as to both the availability of new listings and their potential contribution to trading activity. The need for an adequate flow of new listings by all exchanges is reflected in the historical, downward tendency in share turnover and in the inevitable decline and fall of certain industries and corporations. For regional exchanges, special problems exist. Successful issues periodically graduate to the national exchanges.[32] Because of their small initial volume, moreover, growth is desirable as an end in itself.

During the postwar decade, the annual average of net new listings on the New York Stock Exchange has been slightly in excess of 29.[33] For the period 1947 to 1951, net yearly growth amounted to 48. The prewar peak of 1,308 listings, attained during 1930, was not exceeded, however, until 1947.

Since it is the recognized market place for the issues of leading

[32] This difficulty, it should be noted, also confronts the American Stock Exchange.
[33] New York Stock Exchange, *Year Book,* 1954, p. 32. Net new listings comprise gross additions to listings *minus* delistings.

corporations, the New York Stock Exchange has relatively little difficulty in finding additional listings. The prestige factor alone is sufficient to influence many corporations. Although its reputation does not equal that of the New York Stock Exchange, the American Stock Exchange obtains a steady flow of new common stock listings through active promotion and emphasis upon foreign issues.[34] For the period 1951–1954, the net annual increment in common stocks listed on the American Exchange averaged slightly more than 23. By the beginning of 1955, some 139 of the 826 stocks traded on this exchange were foreign issues.

In contrast, the position of regional exchanges with respect to new listings appears relatively poor. For reasons which are examined subsequently, regional exchanges are confronted with severe competition from the over-the-counter segment of the securities market. The consequence is that a substantial proportion of new listings on regional exchanges comprises stocks of national firms which list regionally as a public relations gesture.

To illustrate the unhappy condition of regional exchanges, let us consider the case of the San Francisco Exchange. Its net yearly increase in listings from 1945 to 1954 has averaged less than 5.[35] Gross annual growth has been slightly in excess of 8 during this period. If regional listing of issues already listed on the New York exchanges is excluded, gross additions average between 1 and 2.

Officials of regional exchanges admit to limited success in obtaining new regional listings. They point out, however, that the encouragement of new listings is only one aspect of the problem. Of equal relevance in several instances is the inability of regional exchanges to keep existing regional listings.

Losses of regional listings appear to be primarily attributable to three factors. Regional stocks graduate to the national exchanges. Corporations whose issues are traded regionally merge with larger companies. Firms are induced to delist their securities so that they may be traded over-the-counter. Although graduation to the national exchanges has historically been the dominant element, the latter two items currently occasion the greatest losses.

Of the New York exchanges, only the American Stock Exchange is appreciably affected by these considerations. The more successful American listings are from time to time transferred to the New York Stock Exchange. Mergers occur between corporations whose issues are listed on the national exchanges. In each case, however,

[34] American Stock Exchange, *President's Report*, 1953–1954, pp. 6–7.
[35] San Francisco Stock Exchange, *Statistical Report*, December 31, 1953, p. 10.

the shares of the surviving firm are increased, and augmented trading ensues.

Through our examination of new listing potential, consideration has been given to a principal effect of recognized position upon total volume and, indirectly, marketability. Here as well as elsewhere, the comparative status of regional exchanges leaves much to be desired.

DIFFERENCES AMONG NATIONAL AND REGIONAL LISTINGS

A related matter meriting attention is the presence of noticeable differences in the quality and diversity of issues traded on the national exchanges and those traded primarily on regional exchanges. A reasonable a priori presumption is that the dominant group(s) of stocks on any given exchange sets the tone of the entire market provided by that exchange and conditions the marketability of all issues traded thereon.

Of major concern in this connection are the dispersion and skewness of security prices on the various exchanges and the intraexchange homogeneity, or absence thereof, of the listings. Significant variations among exchanges in the distribution of stock prices imply the likelihood of dissimilar behavior. Low-priced issues are typically regarded as more volatile and more subject to speculative activity than are medium- or high-priced shares. High-priced stocks are often thought to be characterized by restricted trading activity.

As indicated in chapter ii, organized exchanges are designed to service only a few types of securities. It follows from this that the less homogeneous the securities traded on any given exchange, the less effectively is that exchange likely to function.

The distribution of common stock prices for 14 organized exchanges is disclosed in table 12 for issues traded on February 17, 1955. Included among the 14 exchanges are the New York and American exchanges, 9 regional exchanges, and 3 Canadian exchanges. In the case of the San Francisco and Los Angeles exchanges, issues dually traded on the New York Stock Exchange are listed separately. In the other regional exchanges, all dually listed domestic issues are omitted.

From the data presented in table 12, it can be observed that stocks listed on the New York Stock Exchange are concentrated in the $10 to $50 bracket. Interestingly enough, the great majority of issues traded on the American Exchange fall within the zero to $20 range. With the exception of the Midwest Exchange, regional

TABLE 12

DISTRIBUTION BY PRICE GROUPINGS OF STOCKS TRADED ON 14 EXCHANGES DURING FEBRUARY 17, 1955

Price range (in dollars)	New York	American	San Francisco Also N.Y.	San Francisco Not N.Y.	Los Angeles Also N.Y.	Los Angeles Not N.Y.	Toronto	Montreal[a]	Canadian[a]	Midwest[a]	Boston[a]	Phil.[a]	Cinn.[a]	Detroit[a]	Pitt.[a]	Salt Lake[a]
0–5	17	120	6	23	6	24	121	…	6	6	3	…	1	6	2	33
5–10	51	112	8	11	9	4	25	3	3	9	…	…	…	3	2	…
10–20	184	131	18	20	24	8	17	9	2	14	2	4	…	3	…	…
20–30	206	78	27	9	30	1	12	16	…	13	3	1	…	1	2	…
30–40	169	24	21	3	20	4	9	13	…	6	1	…	1	…	1	…
40–50	135	15	25	4	29	2	4	6	…	5	…	…	2	…	…	…
50–60	83	12	12	3	15	…	3	5	1	2	…	…	1	…	…	…
60–70	52	3	8	2	7	1	3	4	2	4	…	…	…	…	…	…
70–80	40	4	11	3	12	…	1	1	…	…	…	…	…	…	…	…
80–90	28	4	9	1	7	…	1	2	…	…	…	…	1	…	…	…
90–100	16	1	5	3	…	…	…	…	…	…	…	1	…	…	…	…
100 up	36	11	10	3	10	2	2	3	1	…	1	…	…	…	…	…
Total	1,017	515	160	85	172	46	198	62	15	59	10	6	6	13	7	33

SOURCE: *Wall Street Journal*, Pacific Coast edition, February 18, 1955.
[a] Duals excluded.

exchanges resemble the American Exchange in this respect far more closely than they do the New York Stock Exchange.[36]

The localization which characterizes the distribution of stock prices on both the American and regional exchanges first of all requires reconciliation with share turnover data. If speculative activity and low prices go hand in hand, trading volume and share turnover can be expected to move inversely with stock prices.[37] Contrary to these expectations, however, share turnover for the New York Stock Exchange equals that for the American Exchange and exceeds that for the San Francisco Exchange. Of the cases examined, only the Toronto Exchange exhibits the anticipated relationships of higher turnover ratios and lower prices.

The conflicting results suggest several possibilities. They indicate that speculative activity may not be confined to low-priced issues. They imply, in the case of the American Exchange, that foreign stocks may not have their primary market in the United States. They reveal that issues traded principally on regional exchanges may stimulate relatively less interest than those traded on the national exchanges.

The behavior of national listings when splits, mergers, and the like are announced demonstrates that speculative trading is not the sole prerogative of low-priced issues. At best, it is only a tendency which can be outweighed by other factors.

It seems legitimate to suppose that the primary market places are in some instances foreign security exchanges. Evidence supporting this contention is found in the high percentage of Canadian securities among foreign issues listed domestically and in the vitality of Canadian exchanges. More than 70 per cent of the foreign stock issues traded on the American Exchange are Canadian.[38] Canadian exchanges in turn compare favorably with United States' exchanges from the viewpoint of both size and share turnover. In terms of dollar values of transactions for 1953, the Toronto Stock Exchange surpassed the American Exchange, whereas the Montreal and Canadian stock exchanges taken together exceed the Midwest Stock Exchange.[39]

---

[36] The Cincinnati Exchange is ignored because of the paucity of stocks traded thereon.

[37] In view of the possibility that speculative activity is a function of the market level, this relation is presumed to hold only when the market is relatively active and security prices are at or above their normal trend line.

[38] American Stock Exchange, *President's Report*, 1953–1954, p. 6.

[39] Because of the low average price of securities traded on the Canadian exchanges, the physical volume of transactions is not deemed relevant.

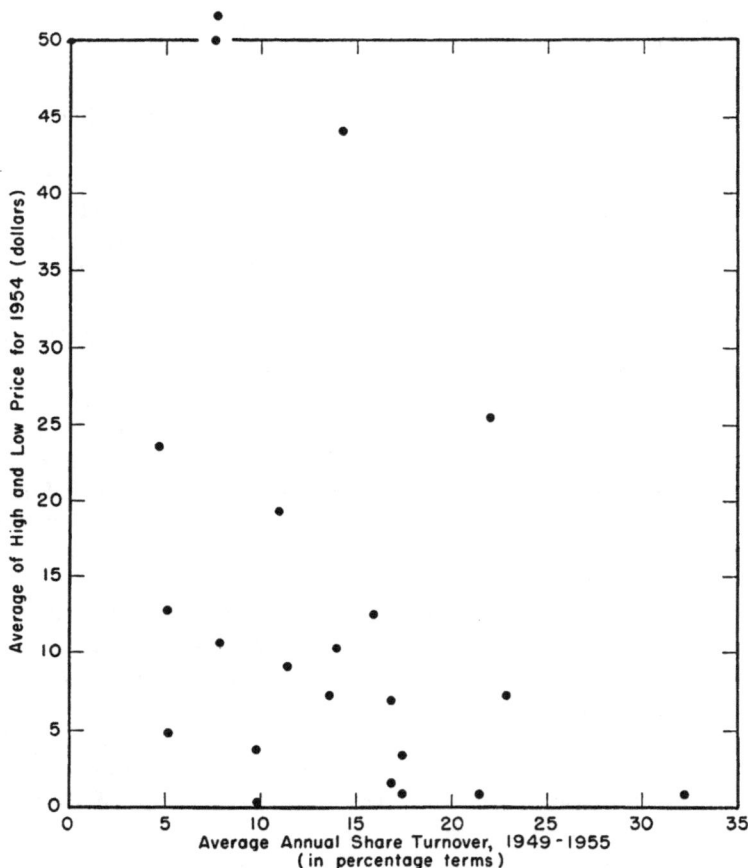

Fig. 2. Relation of share turnover to prices.

In listed and unlisted domestic issues traded on the American Exchange, the degree of market splitting may also be significantly greater than that which ocurs in connection with multiply traded issues listed on the New York Stock Exchange. In some instances, the interest in such stocks may still be largely regional.[40] These considerations, together with differences in both the quality of issues and exchange prestige, appear sufficient to produce the observed turnover relationship.

In order to test the correlation between share turnover and prices of stocks traded primarily on regional exchanges, the sample of 25 San Francisco listings is utilized once more. Figure 2 relates the

[40] Note, for example, tables 2 and 27.

average of the 1954 high and low prices for each issue to its average annual turnover for the period 1949 to 1955. The points are widely scattered and exhibit no definite pattern. Quality variations and other factors apparently rank on a par with security prices in their influence upon share turnover.

As a second step, it is of some interest to ascertain the degree of concentration in security prices, since this may reflect upon both the balance of the exchange and its objectives. Degree of concentration is measured simply by the ratio of issues falling within the dominant price groupings to total issues traded. Although somewhat incomplete, the data contained in table 12 serve as a satisfactory calculating concentration ratios.

The extreme case is represented by the Salt Lake City Exchange with a concentration ratio of 100 per cent. The Los Angeles Exchange possesses a concentration ratio of 78 per cent. The New York and American stock exchanges follow with ratios in the neighborhood of 70 per cent. The San Francisco and Midwest exchanges have ratios which fall in the low sixties.

The effect of variations in the degree of concentration can only be surmised. One possibility is that the larger the concentration ratio, the greater is the influence of the dominant issues (as indicated by price categories) upon the behavior of other stocks. A second is that fluctuations in total activity increase as the degree of concentration rises. A further possibility is that the ability to obtain new listings is affected by the dispersion of security prices.

Whenever a high degree of concentration occurs in the lower price brackets, investor opinions as well as listing attitudes are undoubtedly influenced. Such a condition thus becomes difficult to rectify once it is created.

Closely associated with these considerations are divergencies in issue quality. Low stock prices reflect newness, indifferent success, or even outright failure of the issuing company. If corporations are profitable, the prices of their shares can be expected to rise over time and ultimately, unless offset by stock splits or high dividends payout ratios, to emerge from the low-price category. Concentrations in low-priced issues on regional exchanges indicate, for this reason, the likelihood of significant variations in the quality of stocks traded thereon.

Rough insight into the proportions of low-grade issues traded on the various organized exchanges is obtainable by ascertaining the relative importance of stocks whose issuers refrain from declar-

ing dividends. Omission of dividends may of course be attributed
to diverse causes. Some presumption nonetheless exists that failure
to pay dividends when economic conditions are generally good is
indicative of internal difficulties of one kind or another.

As might be anticipated, the ratio of common stocks paying dividends to total stocks listed is high for the New York Stock Exchange. For both 1952 and 1953, the figure exceeded 90 per cent.[41]
Although information of this type is not reported for the American
Stock Exchange, its 1953–1954 Report states that one-half of the
common stocks traded thereon have paid dividends for ten or more
consecutive years.

Sixty-one common stocks traded on the San Francisco Exchange
paid no cash dividends during 1954, as compared with 51 during
1953.[42] Ratios of nondividend shares to total common stocks traded
on the San Francisco Exchange thus range between 15 and 20 per
cent for this period. The differential between these ratios and those
for the New York Stock Exchange would be increased if issues listed
on the New York Stock Exchange were excluded. For 1954, less
than one-sixth of the nondividend stocks traded on the San Francisco Exchange were listed on the New York Stock Exchange.

The fact that shares traded primarily on regional exchanges often
possess significantly different features than do those traded on the
New York Exchange has interesting implications. It suggests that
the marketing procedures for issues traded on regional exchanges
may be both unduly uniform and patterned too closely after the
national exchanges. It also indicates that comparisons with other
distribution channels, for example, the over-the-counter segment,
may be highly revealing. Each of these matters will be treated in
subsequent chapters.

One further test of market efficacy merits examination. This test
is comparative price behavior. Its introduction has been deferred
until now principally because of what it may reveal in connection
with the impact of dominant stock groupings upon the operation
of regional exchanges.

Variations in security prices depict the degree of risk inherent
in share ownership. Of particular interest are price fluctuations
during periods of economic disturbance. Although stocks characterized by limited trading may perform very well under ordinary
circumstances, doubts arise as to their ability to withstand the vicis-
situdes of depressed conditions.

[41] New York Stock Exchange, *Annual Reports*, 1952, p. 4; and 1953, p. 5.
[42] Of these nonpaying stocks, 7 paid stock dividends in 1954, as did 5 in 1953.

It would of course be tedious to prepare price indexes for each of the major regional exchanges and for the New York exchanges. For this reason, comparative analysis is limited to the New York and San Francisco exchanges. Moody's Index of stock prices is presumed to measure the behavior of listings on the New York Stock

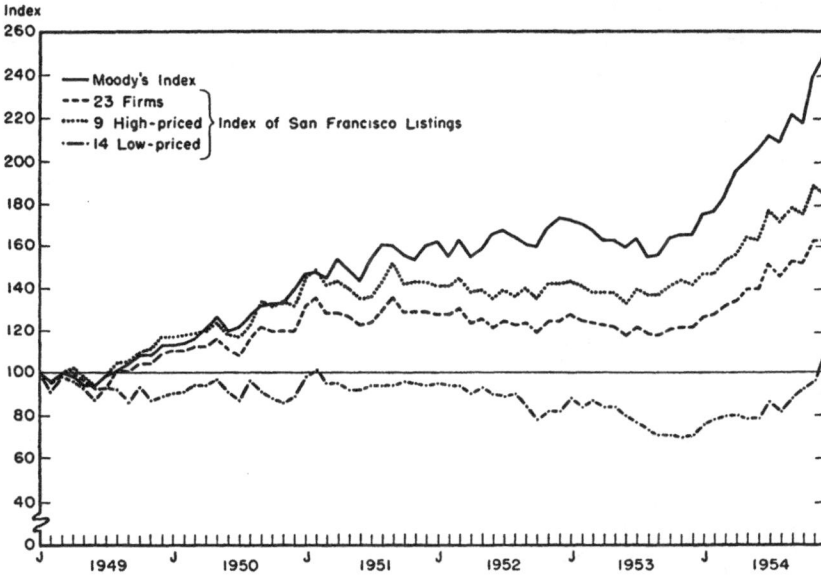

Fig. 3. Comparative indexes of security prices, 1949–1954.

Exchange. To represent the San Francisco Exchange, an index of security prices is constructed, using the sample of 25 issues as the basis.[48]

Figure 3 shows the relationship between Moody's Index and the San Francisco index during the interval January, 1949, to January, 1955. Figure 4 contains a similar comparison for two earlier periods (1937–1938 and 1946) during which the securities market fluctuated significantly. In each instance, the initial month is taken as the base period.

At least two relevant conclusions can be drawn from the comparison of price indexes as exhibited in figures 3 and 4. One is that declines in the prices of regional issues are sharper than those in New York listings. The other is that recovery tends to be slower

---

[48] Because of a lack of continuity in two instances, only 23 issues are employed to prepare the index, covering the period January, 1949, through December, 1954. For 1937, 1938, and 1946, different and slightly smaller samples are utilized.

in regional issues. Both of these behavioral differences support the contention that national listings enjoy superior liquidity. They do not, however, isolate the causes.

In order to ascertain whether dominant price categories exert a noticeable influence, a price index of 14 low-priced San Francisco listings is contrasted with that of 9 high-priced issues in figure 3. Their behavior is noticeably dissimilar throughout the six-year period. Price movements of the high-priced shares parallel Moody's

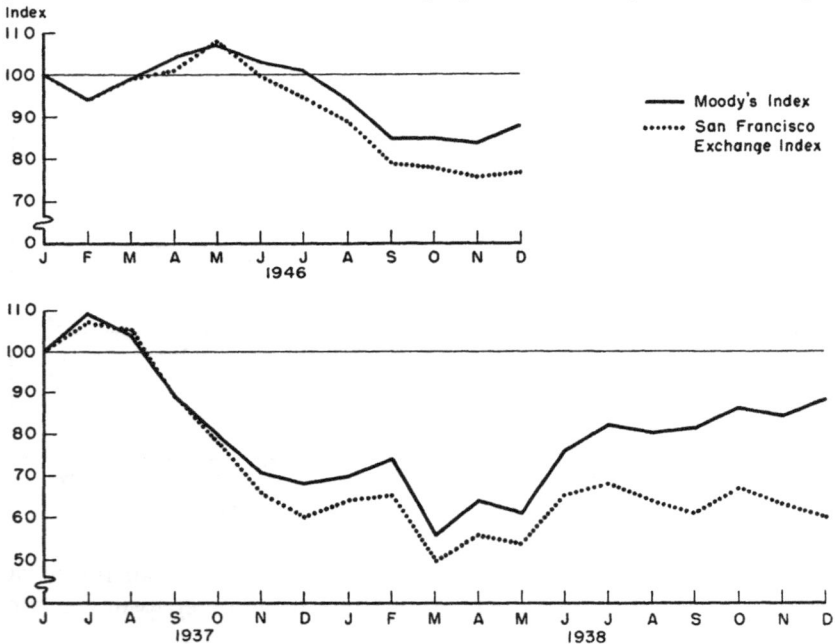

Fig. 4. Comparative indexes of security prices, 1937, 1938, 1946.

Index more closely than they do variations in the low-priced stocks. The implication is that fluctuations in the prices of dominant issues do not necessarily establish the pattern for all stocks traded primarily on the San Francisco Exchange."

CONCLUSIONS

The foregoing comparisons with the national exchanges accentuate the inferior position of most regional exchanges. With reasonably

---

" Based upon the data continued in table 12, low-priced issues are presumed to be the most important grouping. If multiply traded stocks are included, however, no category can be said to predominate. The factor of multiple listings may well influence the observed relationships.

similar procedures for both national and regional exchanges, the underlying cause must be differences in the nature and number of the securities traded. Questions then arise as to what steps are available for altering the nature and number of primary regional listings and/or, if this is insufficient, what adjustments can be made in procedures of regional exchanges.

The principal basis for contrasting the performance of national and regional exchanges is found in the similarity of distribution procedures. The fact that regional issues generally behave less satisfactorily then national listings does not necessarily imply that better markets exist elsewhere for regional issues. Nor does it suggest that any given stock will perform better on the New York exchanges than on the regional exchanges. With respect to this latter point, James Day of the Midwest Exchange makes the unchallenged contention that Bliss and Laughlins, Noblett Sparks, and about 100 other such stocks did not improve their status by listing on the New York Stock Exchange.[45]

---

[45] J. R. Elliot, Jr., "Regional Exchanges," *Barrons* (June 27, 1955), p. 28.

IV

Measuring the Effectiveness of Regional Exchanges: Evaluation by Absolute Criteria

The success of any distribution channel depends upon its ability to provide satisfactory salability and price stability within the limits set by the attributes of the assets traded.[1] Specification of *absolute* criteria for determining the achievements of regional security exchanges in this regard is by no means simple. It involves the enumeration and interpretation of those factors which reflect in some fashion the contribution of regional exchanges to the liquidity of listed shares.

Evaluation of factors affecting liquidity is especially troublesome. The selection of minimum standards and the assignment of weights to the individual items are largely matters of judgment. Limitations imposed by the attributes of the asset traded frequently cannot be adequately distinguished from those associated with the exchange itself. That is to say, unsatisfactory performance on the part of regional exchanges may simply indicate a failure to attract qualified regional issues. As a further point, there still remains the question of relative effectiveness even though the contribution of regional exchanges to the liquidity of regional issues is deemed to be positive.

In spite of these difficulties, it is legitimate to ask whether stocks traded on regional exchanges are characterized by reasonable transactions volume, continuity of trading, and so on. This, after all, is all that the formulation and utilization of absolute criteria purports to accomplish. At the very least, some impression can be gained of the general adequacy of regional exchanges.

[1] The term "liquidity" is interpreted in its broader sense to encompass both salability or marketability and price stability or market risk.

MIDWEST EXCHANGE STUDIES

Market studies conducted by the Midwest Stock Exchange provide an appropriate point of departure for the analysis at hand. The orientation of these studies, as distinct from ours, seems to be one of accepting the procedures of organized exchanges as given and of investigating the characteristics of stocks whose marketing requirements conform at least reasonably well to these procedures.[2] Although primary consideration is given to stocks traded on the Chicago (Midwest) Exchange, almost every issue traded on the New York, Boston, Los Angeles, San Francisco, and Chicago stock exchanges is reported to have been reviewed.

The technique utilized is to state arbitrarily that the minimum requisite activity for any local issue is an average of 100 shares per trading day and to differentiate stocks on this basis. In each instance, share volume is related to such factors as number of shares outstanding, number of shares held in large blocks, price per share, par value as affecting the amount of tax paid on sales, degree of public acceptance or knowledge of the company and its products, and location of the company in relation to the exchange. Characteristics normally associated with the more active issues become the basis for setting minimum standards.

CONCLUSIONS AND EVALUATION

On the basis of observed patterns, officials of the Midwest Exchange conclude that an orderly and serviceable market can normally be maintained with a projected volume of 25,000 shares annually on a minimum-sized issue of 150,000 shares in the hands of the public and held by 750 to 1,000 stockholders.[3] Listing with organized exchanges is also believed to benefit many issues which feature an even smaller annual volume. The criterion employed in such cases is the existence of consistent quotations for such stocks at reasonable spreads.

Little need be said about the validity of the suggested criteria

[2] Information concerning these studies is obtained from R. Thorson, "The Midwest Stock Exchange," *Analysts Journal*, X, no. 1 (Feb., 1954), pp. 57-59, and from correspondence with Carl E. Ogren, vice-president and secretary of the Midwest Stock Exchange. The initial study dealt with the 1944-1945 period. Several supplementary surveys are said to have been made since that time.

[3] These minimum standards, obtained from the article by R. Thorson, are slightly lower and somewhat less comprehensive than those currently endorsed by the Midwest Exchange. Officials of the Midwest Exchange recommend further that standards be elevated wherever prices per share exceed moderate levels, say $25, and that stocks feature low par values. The purpose of the latter is to minimize transfer taxes.

other than to point out that the 100-share-per-trading-day figure (i.e., annual volume of 25,000 shares) is not explicitly defended and that the performance of similar issues in over-the-counter channels is not examined. Although a yearly volume of 25,000 shares may be adequate under ordinary circumstances, the real test is behavior under extraordinary conditions. The market for any security whose depth approximates 100 shares per trading day can readily absorb neither sizable individual transactions nor significant clusterings of normal-sized orders to buy or sell.

It may, in addition, be argued that a study of this type considers but one aspect of the problem. For the investing public, the performance of regional exchanges relative to alternative marketing channels is of equal importance. Even though organized exchanges provide satisfactory markets for issues with an annual volume of 25,000 shares, over-the-counter trading may occasion both higher and more stable net prices.[4]

APPLICATION TO REGIONAL EXCHANGES

Since the minimum volume figure of 25,000 shares presumably expresses the reasoned opinion of the Midwest Stock Exchange, some weight should undoubtedly be attached thereto. Annual summaries of transactions for the San Francisco and Midwest exchanges are therefore examined to determine the number of issues failing to meet this standard. In the San Francisco Exchange, some 286 issues feature a volume of 25,000 or less in 1953, as compared with 260 in 1954. These amount to between 70 and 80 per cent of the total stocks traded on this exchange.[5] In the Midwest Exchange, some 219 issues failed to surpass the 25,000-share level in 1954. This comprises more than 55 per cent of total issues traded thereon.

The situation in regional exchanges, fortunately, is not as bad as these magnitudes seem to indicate. The elimination of preferred stocks, whose activity is normally substantially below that of common stocks, reduces somewhat the relative proportions of substandard issues. Some 42 of the 45 preferred issues traded on the San Francisco Exchange during 1954, for example, had an annual volume of less than 25,000 shares. As far as the Midwest Exchange is concerned, the fact that odd-lot trading is not taken into account conditions the results. Whether the omission of multiply traded issues would alter the relationships appreciably, however, is doubtful.

[4] The term "net" is employed to allow for differences in commissions or spreads.
[5] A similar percentage relationship is observed for the Los Angeles Stock Exchange.

TABLE 13
DISTRIBUTION OF RELATIVE SPREADS FOR UNTRADED ISSUES ON THE
SAN FRANCISCO AND LOS ANGELES EXCHANGES
(in per cent)

Dates	Total untraded issues	Number of untraded issues having relative spreads			
		0–5	5–10	10–20	20 and more
SAN FRANCISCO STOCK EXCHANGE					
1954					
Oct. 12.................	59	25	13	13	8
Nov. 12.................	52	23	11	12	6
Dec. 14.................	67	32	17	13	5
1955					
Jan. 12.................	51	27	10	10	4
Feb. 14.................	51	23	17	9	2
Total...............	280	130	68	57	25
LOS ANGELES STOCK EXCHANGE					
1954					
Oct. 12.................	19	10	2	3	4
Nov. 12.................	14	6	3	4	1
Dec. 14.................	12	9	1	1	1
1955					
Jan. 12.................	8	5	1	1	1
Feb. 14.................	17	7	3	2	5
Total...............	70	37	10	11	12

SOURCE: *Wall Street Journal*, Pacific Coast edition.

Despite these adjustments, the number of *inactive* issues appears large. It thus becomes interesting to consider the question of the spreads between bid and asked prices quoted by specialists. The narrowness and consistency of these spreads determine, in the opinion of Midwest Exchange officials, at least in part whether organized exchanges render a service to the less active issues.

As evidenced by table 11, the ratio of spreads to bid prices is rather high for untraded issues on the San Francisco and Los Angeles exchanges. As shown in table 13 the distribution of relative spreads for untraded stocks on these two exchanges is characterized by considerable dispersion. Although some concentration is observed in the 0–5 per cent range, relative spreads exceed 10 per cent in almost one-third of the cases.

The dispersion reflected in table 13 seems to be affected by the number of low-priced issues, by quality variation, and by relative activity. The influence of low-priced stocks is indicated by the fact that only one of the inactive San Francisco listings whose percentage spread exceeded 20 per cent has a price in excess of $5. The effect of quality variation is suggested by the fact that such issues as Anglo California and Wells Fargo have spreads amounting to less than 3 per cent of bid prices. The impact of relative activity is implied in the tendency—for the San Francisco Exchange at least—for relative spreads to vary in accordance with the number of times they appear in the untraded lists.

As a final point, consistency of spreads does not appear to be an overwhelming virtue of inactive issues. The percentage spreads of approximately half of the San Francisco listings which failed to be traded twice or more jumped classes (table 13) once or more. The implication is therefore that, if standards set by the Midwest Exchange are accepted, regional exchanges fail to render substantial benefits to a significant number of regional listings.[6]

FACTORS INFLUENCING SALABILITY

Whether or not agreement is reached as to specific standards, the Midwest studies correctly emphasize volume. Trading activity conditions in large part the salability of listed issues. It is not, however, the sole consideration. Questions pertaining to the continuity of trading, the relationship between individual orders and daily trading volume, absorption potential (as evidenced by other considerations), and trading activity during adverse periods also arise.

TRADING CONTINUITY

Trading continuity, as related to individual issues, can be measured by ratios of days in which no trading occurs to total trading days. A reasonable degree of continuity is presumed to imply that transactions will take place at least three to four days out of each trading week. That is to say, the proportion of days not traded to total trading days should not exceed 20 to 40 per cent.

The basis for this conclusion is threefold. Inactivity dissipates

---

[6] The possibility that the difficulties may be inherent in the stock rather than in the exchange is not denied. If such is the case, however, interesting questions arise as to the effectiveness of listing and delisting procedures.

TABLE 14
YEARLY PERCENTAGE OF DAYS NOT TRADED TO TOTAL
TRADING DAYS IN 1953 FOR 25 ISSUES
(251 trading days)

Listing corporation	Ratio of days not traded to total trading days
Menasco	57.0
Morr. Knudsen	55.0
Westates Common	53.8
Calaveras	52.2
West. Dept. Stores	50.6
Emporium–Capwell	49.4
General Paint	44.6
Atok Big-Wedge	43.8
El Dorado	39.0
Marchant	38.6
S & W FF	37.1
Westates Pfd	36.3
Anglo California	32.3
Intex Oil	29.1
Matson	25.5
Pacific Coast Agg.	24.7
Golden State	23.9
Central Eureka	20.3
Dominguez Oil	16.3
Palmer Stendel[a]	15.8
Oceanic Oil	15.6
Hawaiian Pineapple	15.1
Id.-Md.	8.8
Blair Holdings	6.4
MJM and M	1.2

SOURCE: Records of the San Francisco Stock Exchange.
[a] First traded April 9, 1955—184 days.

one of the principal advantages of listing, that is, publicity. The absence of continuous markets further implies that the cost of acquisition or disposition is often greater than would otherwise be the case.[7] In addition, whether valid or not, lack of continuity suggests lack of salability to many investors.

[7] If orders to buy are matched against orders to sell, the principal cost to the buyer and seller is the brokerage commission. If no matching occurs, as is usual where noncontinuous markets exist, a part of the spread should be regarded as an element of

In order to examine the continuity of activity in stocks traded primarily on regional exchanges, attention is again directed to the sample of 25 leading issues traded primarily on the San Francisco Exchange. For each stock, the percentage ratio of days not traded to total trading days is derived for 1953 and is shown in table 14. Of the 25 issues, the ratios of 8 exceed 40 per cent, and those of 18 surpass 20 per cent.

Although ratios of days not traded to total trading days are exhibited in table 14 for only one year, the relationships are not greatly different for other years. The consequence is that, since these represent leading issues in terms of trading volume, the San Francisco Exchange at least does not rank too well in trading continuity.

IMPORTANCE OF INDIVIDUAL TRANSACTIONS

Salability, as it pertains to issues of stock, presupposes not only trading continuity, but also suitable relationships between individual transactions and daily trading volume. The reason is simply that market perfection requires numerous buyers and sellers per unit of time, each acquiring or disposing of relatively insignificant amounts.[8] In spite of their failure to take into account the possibility of close substitutes, ratios of single transactions to daily volume in individual issues provide some insight into the degree of market perfection.

Regional exchanges fare rather poorly in this respect. For the Midwest, San Francisco, and Los Angeles exchanges, average daily trading is less than 200 shares per issue. When this figure is considered in the light of the minimum round-lot order, that is, 100 shares, it becomes apparent that the average ratio of individual transactions to daily trading is extremely high.

To test this relationship further, individual transactions on the San Francisco Exchange are examined for March 4, 1955.[9] For the 115 issues traded on that day, the over-all ratio of "normal-sized" (most frequent) orders to daily activity amounts to slightly more than 60 per cent. In 52 instances, single transactions occur, thus

---

the acquisition or disposition cost. If the price, where matching occurs, falls midway between the bid and asked quotation, this additional cost is equal to one-half the spread. Since the spread is influenced by the risk to the specialist, moveover, limited activity is likely to be associated with relatively high spreads.

[8] Here as well as elsewhere, the appropriate time period is presumed to be the "trading day."

[9] Source of data is San Francisco Stock Exchange, *Daily Transactions*, March 4, 1955. Round-lot transactions only are considered.

producing a percentage ratio of 100 per cent. In 85 cases, the ratio of "maximum-sized" orders to daily trading is 50 per cent or more.

The undue importance of single transactions expressed in relative terms affects both salability and price stability unless counteracted by other considerations. On the one hand, the market apparently cannot readily absorb large buy or sell orders. On the other hand, decisions to buy or sell by a few traders may significantly alter the flow of orders. The consequence is that either sizable individual orders (or abnormal clusterings of orders in one direction) cannot be executed or substantial price adjustments are required to induce sufficient interest to permit their execution.

One saving feature for regional exchanges may well be that investors implicitly recognize this difficulty in their decisions to buy or sell regional issues. That is to say, regional exchanges are rarely put to severe tests. Little of course can be done about forced liquidations except—where they are sufficiently large—to make use of secondary distributions. Another compensative factor, which is discussed below, may be the existence of close substitutes.

ABSORPTION POTENTIAL

By virtue of their simplicity and their concern with events which have actually transpired, objective measures of the type just examined leave something to be desired. The fact that trading has occurred indicates merely that the highest bid matched the lowest offer or that the specialist interceded. It does not—without further analysis—reveal the readiness of investors and specialists to acquire or dispose of shareholdings in accordance with changes in the price structure. Nor does it reflect the salability of issues which, for reasons of concentrated ownership and/or class of investor, are ordinarily characterized by infrequent transfers of shares.

To resolve these difficulties, the concept of *absorption potential* is introduced. Let it be understood that absorption potential refers to the ability of the market to distribute, without significant price adjustments, increments to the shares of any given stock which are offered for sale. Let it be further understood that the analysis of absorption potential is designed to supplement, rather than to encompass, the preceding discussion.

The failure of trading volume and continuity to show absorption potential is particularly noticeable in the case of high quality, defensive stocks which attract long-term investors. For low-volume quality issues, such as Pacific Telephone and Telegraph (common and preferred), Southern California Gas (preferred), and Wells Fargo, ratios of spreads quoted by specialists to market prices are frequently 2 per cent or less.[10] Narrow spreads imply confidence on the part of specialists that positions can be adjusted without undue risk; that is, that buyers or sellers can be located if the need arises.

Interpretation of ratios of individual to daily transactions is subject to analogous limitations. High ratios may result from a restricted supply of shares offered for sale, as well as from a variety of other factors. Under such conditions, the nature of the demand curves for the issues in question assumes relevance. Assuming the demands to be highly elastic, that is, the demand curves to be approximately horizontal over wide ranges, high ratios need not be inconsistent with substantial absorption potential.

The absorption potential of the market for any given stock depends largely upon the quantity of close substitutes in existence. Assume, for purposes of illustration, a collection of stocks ($a, b, \ldots, n$) which are approximately identical in the opinion of the investing public. Assume further that an increased flow of orders to sell stock a depresses its market price. Since stock a is now relatively cheap, the holders of stock ($b, c, \ldots, n$) switch to stock a until the price structure is once more in balance. The process resembles that of arbitrage to a striking degree.

The fact that securities are essentially claims to income, differentiated on the basis of risk, suggests that an ample number of close, and perhaps even of perfect, substitutes is available. Close substitutes may be defined as those issues belonging to a given risk classification, whereas perfect substitutes can be viewed as claims to income characterized by identical, or approximately identical, risk.[11] Although the lines of demarcation among risk categories are indefinite, grouping of securities on the basis of low, medium, and high risk is permissible and conforms to investor thinking.

Despite their underlying similarity, the observed behavior of individual stocks indicates that the range of substitutes is affected by other considerations as well and may be exceedingly restricted

---

[10] The issues to which reference is made are regional listings on the San Francisco Exchange.

[11] Wherever perfect or near-perfect substitutes are present, a good case can be made for reconstituting ratios of individual to daily transactions to reveal this fact. The necessary adjustment consists of combining the daily transactions for all stocks thus related. This step is not taken in the present analysis because of the difficulty involved in ascertaining which issues are sufficiently close substitutes to be treated together.

in many regional issues. Among the more important factors is imperfect knowledge. Investors are often unaware of the alternatives open to them.

Both industry lines and market subdivisions tend to erect further barriers which interfere with substitution relationships among securities. Not only does the degree of risk associated with shares of stock depend upon their industrial classification, but also changes in the interpretation of risk are likely to proceed along industry lines.[12] Market subdivisions exert an analogous impact so far as their status influences investor attitudes. The areas encompassed by distribution channels are also relevant, since they determine in large part the trading areas for the various issues.

Trading areas for regional listings are conditioned by the fact that members of the appropriate regional exchanges have the principal incentive to promote interest in such securities. Except where the possibility of either reciprocity or active over-the-counter trading exists, nonmember brokerage firms have little reason to recommend the acquisition of regional listings.[13] The consequence is that the amount of potentially close substitutes for any regional listing is likely to be confined to other listings on the same exchange (including those with unlisted trading privileges) and to over-the-counter issues traded within the market span of the regional exchange in question.

As evidenced by the distribution of regional offerings for the Los Angeles and San Francisco exchanges shown in tables 18 and 19, regional exchanges are characterized neither by balanced offerings nor, with minor exceptions, by an appreciable depth in regional offerings of any particular kind. The principal exception to this, as far as West Coast exchanges are concerned, arises in connection with petroleum stocks which appear to have adequate depth. To the extent that close substitutes are confined to particular industries and to media traded in a given segment of the securities market, therefore, the quantity of close substitutes for most regional listings appears to be small.

It is true that the offerings of regional exchanges are augmented substantially by the presence of multiply traded issues. Substitution between this group and regional stocks nonetheless may be limited

---

[12] That is to say, even when the securities market as a whole is relatively stable, there may—for one reason or another—be considerable investor interest in steels and little activity in, say, retail trade.

[13] The Los Angeles and San Francisco exchanges do, of course, offer discounts of 25 per cent on commission charges to nonmember firms.

and may, in many instances, be a one-way street. The crucial consideration is whether noncompeting groups of investors assume any degree of importance. Although individual shareholdings are not likely to be restricted to regional offerings, it is reasonable to suppose that investors frequently limit their holdings to nationally known stocks.

Some substitution undoubtedly occurs between regional listings and regional over-the-counter issues. Differences in publicity and marketing techniques between the two channels appear, however, to circumscribe substitution relationships markedly.

As might be anticipated, there is no effective way of measuring the volume of close substitutes for any given regional listing. It can be said that regional listings are distinctly inferior in this respect to nationally listed stocks. It can be also said that the quantity of close substitutes for regional listings is likely to vary with the level of security prices and activity on regional exchanges. Evidence that such may be the case is found in the comparative price behavior of national and regional listings.

Other factors which influence absorption potential and which are inadequately reflected in trading continuity and in relative magnitudes of individual transactions include the possibility of chain reactions and the extent of specialist activity. By "chain reaction" is meant that activity begets activity. So far as traders rely upon transactions volume as a gauge of short-term profit possibilities, abrupt variations in the volume of trading in individual issues can be expected to arouse the interest of those attracted by the prospect of speculative gains.

Partial, though inconclusive, confirmation of the existence of chain reactions may be found by observing intra-annum variations in the activity of individual issues. Although substantial month-to-month changes occur in share volume, a careful examination of these fluctuations is not deemed worthwhile because of the very indefiniteness of the results.[14] Insight into the wide range of variation that is likely to take place can be obtained, however, from the interannum movements in yearly turnover of outstanding shares for 25 San Francisco listings shown in table 8.

The matter of specialist activity has already been treated at some length. Suffice it to say that the effectiveness with which specialists

---

[14] If it were made, such an analysis would presumably involve the calculation of percentage deviations from average monthly trading for individual issues. Relative deviations from average monthly trading for the exchange as a whole might be utilized as the basis for comparison.

execute their market maintenance function appreciably affects the short-run absorption potential for any stock. The principal tool for measuring the effectiveness of specialist activity in absolute terms appears to be the level of, and variation in, relative spreads.

The differential between bid and asked quotations for listed securities reflects the specialists' interpretation of the risk involved in assuming positions in these issues.[15] This differential, commonly referred to as the *spread,* depends upon the quality, concentration in shareholdings (as reflected in share activity and the depth of the specialist's book), and price of the stock in question; the risk associated with the distribution procedures of the exchange on which the security is traded; and the performance of the specialist to which the issue is assigned. To eliminate the effect of variations in price upon differentials, ratios of spreads to bid, asked, or average prices must be employed. Although the size of these ratios, that is, relative spreads, is influenced by several factors, they are nonetheless useful as a rough gauge of specialist willingness to maintain satisfactory markets.

Appendix table B-1 shows the percentage ratio of spreads between ending bid and asked quotations to final bids for all regional San Francisco listings as of the approximate mid-points of October and December, 1954, and March, 1955. Percentage ratios of average deviations from the averages of these relative spreads to the average relative spreads are exhibited in Appendix table B-2. In interpreting these data, either high percentage spreads or, preferably, combinations of large spreads and sizable deviations (both expressed in relative terms) are presumed to indicate less than satisfactory performance on the part of specialists. Because of the technique utilized, large percentage deviations, when associated with low spreads, need not reflect poor performance.

The position is arbitrarily taken that relative spreads in excess of 10 per cent are unduly high for issues whose price per share is normally less than $5. For those stocks whose price per share customarily equals or exceeds $5, the point of demarcation is assumed to be 5 per cent. The basis for distinguishing between *very* low-priced issues and all others is the negative correlation observed between percentage spreads and security prices. As reflected in Appendix table B-1, the most significant change appears to occur between the zero to $5 and the $5 to $10 classes.

---

[15] As in over-the-counter transactions, quoted spreads may be shaded from time to time in the actual execution of orders. The frequency with which this is done is not known.

The justification for selecting relative spreads of 10 and 5 per cent as the dividing points is found in the behavior of spreads for over-the-counter issues. According to studies made at the University of Pennsylvania, the typical ratio of spreads to average prices for over-the-counter issues selling under $20 is 10 per cent, as contrasted with 5 per cent for stocks whose price equals or exceeds $20.[16] In the event that spreads quoted by specialists on regional listings approach those on small-sized over-the-counter transactions, the case for listing becomes one of dubious merit.

For the dates examined, approximately half of the San Francisco listings selling for less than $5 per share have average relative spreads of 10 per cent or more. Almost three-eighths of those selling for $5 or more per share have spreads of 5 per cent and more. Needless to say, these are significant proportions and reflect upon the effectiveness of the specialist function. The figures exclude, moreover, those instances in which no bid or asked quotations are given.

Some one-third of the San Francisco listings in the zero to $5 group possesses average deviations in excess of 25 per cent and spreads of 10 per cent or more.[17] In contrast, roughly two-ninths of those in the $5 and more category feature average deviations in excess of 25 per cent and spreads of 5 per cent or greater. When significant variations are associated with high spreads, the numbers of issues are noticeably reduced, but still of some consequence.

Although less objective than the analysis of trading continuity and relations between individual and daily transactions, the examination of absorption potential does not imply radically different conclusions. In some instances the salability of regional listings may be substantially greater than that suggested by trading continuity and the relative magnitude of individual transactions. In the majority of cases, however, the absorption potential of regional exchanges for regional listings appears to be smaller than might be anticipated.

BEHAVIOR DURING ADVERSE PERIODS

Salability is not a timeless concept. It can be expected to vary as the level of security prices rises and falls. For this reason, attention is focused upon the marketability of regional listings as evidenced

---

[16] I. Friend, M. Hamburg, and S. Schor, *Pricing and Price Differentials on Over-the-Counter Markets* (Philadelphia: University of Pennsylvania Press, 1955), p. 18.

[17] Whether average deviations in excess of 25 per cent are considered to be unduly large or whether some other figure is chosen is principally a question of judgment.

by trading indexes, share turnover, and ratios of days not traded to total trading days during adverse periods. The intention is to demonstrate that the conclusions drawn from relatively current data hold equally well (if not more so) under less favorable circumstances.

On a priori grounds, trading volume in periods of declining or abnormally low stock prices need not be consistently high or low. If shareholders desire to liquidate their holdings and are willing (or forced) to do so whatever the price, substantial trading may ensue. If shareholders wish to sell, but in general insist upon reasonable prices, few transactions may result.

It can be said on an a priori basis that variations in salability are not wholly divorced from changes in security prices. The flow of orders both to buy and sell stocks is affected by prevailing and expected prices. As the flow diminishes and/or the relation between buy and sell orders becomes unbalanced, marketability decreases. This proposition follows from the fact that market perfection requires large numbers of buyers and sellers.

Indexes of annual share volume furnish a useful, general measure of marketability. Although subject to limitations, their utilization permits comparison of interperiod changes in transactions volume and thereby facilitates the uncovering of uniformities of pattern— if they exist. Indexes (1953 = 100) of annual activity on the New York, American, and San Francisco exchanges are shown in table 15 for the years 1920 to 1955.

The data contained in table 15 reveal that physical volume of trading is for the most part positively correlated with the level of the market from year to year.[18] The principal exception to the observed pattern is the behavior of trading activity on the San Francisco Exchange during 1946. In that year, volume rose significantly over 1945 despite declines in stock prices.

The atypical performance of trading on the San Francisco Exchange in 1946 can perhaps be explained in terms of the fact that the market break did not occur until the latter months of the year. As late as July, 1946, Moody's Index of stock prices exceeded its January level. Although the indexes of trading on the New York

---

[18] There is no presumption that this correlation holds equally well for day-to-day and month-to-month fluctuations in stock prices. Nor is this statement intended to imply that minor variations in stock prices from year to year are always associated with corresponding changes in share activity. Since long-term influences upon prices and volume assume importance as the time span is extended, comparisons between years which are separated by intervals of, say, five years or more are likely to be misleading.

TABLE 15

INDEXES OF SHARE VOLUME FOR ISSUES TRADED ON THE NEW YORK, AMERICAN, AND
SAN FRANCISCO STOCK EXCHANGES FOR THE YEARS 1920–1955
(1953 = 100)

Year	Exchange		
	San Francisco	New York	American[a]
1920	10.72	64.1	.....
1921	9.15	48.7	15.2
1922	16.39	73.5	21.2
1923	34.29	66.6	49.8
1924	39.2	80.0	70.6
1925	54.2	129.6	86.3
1926	55.6	127.3	112.8
1927	64.9	163.9	122.2
1928	180.0	262.3	236.6
1929	109.8	317.0	465.1
1930	87.3	228.4	217.1
1931	56.6	162.6	107.8
1932	40.4	119.8	55.8
1933	46.6	184.6	98.6
1934	26.6	91.3	58.7
1935	44.2	107.6	74.0
1936	51.2	139.8	131.7
1937	39.6	115.4	101.8
1938	37.4	83.8	48.5
1939	36.1	73.8	44.7
1940	34.4	58.5	41.9
1941	27.6	48.1	33.9
1942	19.4	35.4	21.8
1943	30.4	78.6	69.7
1944	34.7	74.1	69.4
1945	55.8	106.4	140.0
1946	85.6	102.5	134.1
1947	61.6	71.5	70.7
1948	69.6	85.2	73.3
1949	59.0	76.7	64.7
1950	82.3	147.9	105.3
1951	104.9	125.0	109.0
1952	104.8	95.2	103.8
1953	100.0	100.0	100.0
1954	93.2	161.5	159.1

SOURCE: New York Stock Exchange, *1954 Year Book;* Records of the San Francisco Stock Exchange;
American Stock Exchange, *President's Report,* 1953–54 and earlier.
[a] Formerly, the New York Curb Exchange.

and American exchanges declined between 1945 and 1946, the decreases are not appreciable.

Though inconclusive, the general pattern exhibited by these indexes is consistent with the hypothesis that the salability of stocks traded on organized exchanges varies directly with the economic climate. This relationship, it may be observed, is of greater importance to regional exchanges than to the national exchanges. The point is that trading on regional exchanges, expressed on a per issue basis, is comparatively light even during active periods. As a result of the low base of transactions, the diminished volume of trading in regional listings associated with adverse periods can be ill afforded.

More refined indicators of trading activity, such as annual share turnover, behave in a manner which parallels the movements of trading indexes. Annual share turnover ratios for 20 leading issues traded principally on the San Francisco Exchange are shown in table 16 for the years 1937, 1938, and 1946.[19] The median ratios approximate 30 per cent for 1937, 10 per cent for 1938, and 20 per cent for 1946.

Both the distribution and interperiod variation of individual ratios suggest that the median ratios are reasonably indicative of comparative turnover levels. In 18 instances, turnover ratios exhibit decreases between 1937 and 1938. For those cases in which comparisons are possible, turnover ratios for 1946 are generally above those for 1938 and exceed those for 1937 in 4 of 7 cases. The behavior of annual turnover ratios for these years apparently reflects the fact that movements in stock prices during 1946 parallel those during 1937 more closely than during 1938. In 1937, as well as 1946, a market break occurs in the latter part of the year.

The examination of recent turnover relationships (table 8) provides further information as to their behavior during adverse periods. Of primary interest is the divergence of 1949 ratios from those for succeeding years. Not only were stock prices relatively low throughout 1949, as contrasted with their subsequent levels, but also a recession in the economy was associated with a break of limited magnitude in the stock market.

In two-thirds of the cases shown in table 8, the turnover ratios for 1949 are below the average for 1949 to 1955. In almost three-tenths of the cases, the 1949 relationships are the lowest of the entire period. In only one-sixth of the cases are they the highest.

---

[19] Selection is based upon the level of transactions volume for the years in question.

The conclusion is that the observed pattern is consistent with that witnessed in 1937 and 1938.

Because of the historical tendency for annual share turnover to decline, it is not deemed worthwhile to look backward beyond 1937.[20] As a matter of fact, comparisons between the 1937–1938 and 1946 data and the 1949–1955 data possess relatively little utility for this and other reasons. For those issues whose turnover ratios are calculated for each of the three periods, the 1937, 1938, and 1946 turnover figures equal or exceed the average of the 1949 to 1955 ratios as general rule.

Ratios of days not traded to total trading days are now introduced to measure interperiod variations in trading continuity. As exhibited in table 17, the 1938 days-not-traded ratios for 20 San Francisco listings exceed 50 per cent in the great majority of instances and, with rare exceptions, are above the 1937 ratios.[21] Concentration in the 50 per cent and over brackets is noticeably greater for 1937 and 1938 than for 1946 and 1953.

Distributions of days-not-traded ratios, shown in table 17, appear consistent with the proposition that trading continuity is positively correlated with the level of the market. Contrary to the pattern of annual share turnover ratios, this relationship holds for comparisons between 1937–1938 and 1946 and 1953, as well as between successive years. The level of 1937 ratios relative to those for 1946 and 1953 can be explained in terms of the fact that the 1937 ratios relate only to the last seven months of that year. The low days-not-traded ratios for 1953 reflect the fact that stock prices in that year fluctuated irregularly at a substantially higher plane than in 1946.

The impression gained from the foregoing data is that marketability of regional listings is affected by the state of the securities market, as measured by, say, indexes of stock prices. If this is true, deficiencies which have been observed in the analysis of current data become more noticeable in adverse periods.

MARKET RISK ASSOCIATED WITH REGIONAL EXCHANGES

In turning to the second aspect of liquidity, that is, price stability, the point is reëmphasized that the liquidity which characterizes any given asset is conditioned by both the kind of asset and the

---

[20] See, for example, New York Stock Exchange, *1953 Year Book,* pp. 32–33.

[21] To eliminate the influence of the market rise during early 1937, the 1937 days-not-traded ratios are calculated for the last seven months only. As a result, they are higher than would otherwise be the case.

nature of the market in which it is bought and sold. It is conceivable that distribution channels whose effectiveness—based upon observed behavior—is questionable may be doing as well as can be reasonably expected in the light of the trading media.

Application of this consideration to the matter of price stability suggests that the risk associated with the asset itself ought to be divorced from that connected with the market. The risk attached to issues of stock is neither uniform among stocks nor constant through time. It varies among stocks in accordance with such factors as the size and financial condition of the issuing company and the characteristics of the industry (or industries) to which the issuer belongs. It changes over time in accordance with the position of the issuing company and with the corporation's prospects for the future.

The effect of risk variations among issues and through time is twofold. In the first place, risky issues are relatively susceptible to changes in investors' psychology. The interest in, and evaluation of, issues of this type can thus be expected to fluctuate widely. Second, increases or decreases in risk, whether real or assumed, from period to period occasion corresponding (but opposite) changes in price-earnings ratios. The consequence is that, wherever the risk associated with the security is considerable, price instability may ensue even under the best of distribution procedures.

Market risk, as related to regional exchanges, is occasioned by inadequate volume (i.e., thinness), undue amounts of speculative activity, unbalanced offerings, inappropriate marketing techniques, and other items. Thin markets impair stability by reducing the ability of markets to absorb variations in the flow of buy or sell orders without significant prices changes.[22] Speculative trading whose economic function is to stabilize prices through time may operate in reverse, provided it results in an excessive bunching of buy or sell orders. Unbalanced offerings augment the vulnerability of regional exchanges, and, in extreme cases, dominant groups are likely to influence the behavior of all listings. Last but not least, inappropriate distribution procedures contribute to risk by fostering thin markets and limited offerings.

The degree of market risk featured by regional exchanges can be measured indirectly by establishing the importance of these risk determinants and directly by examining the behavior of price-

---

[22] An unduly thin market may of course be ascribable to the fact that a corporation is closely held or has a limited number of shares outstanding, as well as to the characteristics of the market.

TABLE 16

ANNUAL TURNOVER RATIOS FOR LEADING SAN FRANCISCO LISTINGS

Listing company	Years		Listing company	Year
	1937	1938		1946
Union Sugar................	64.20	15.85	Intex Oil................	78.6
Marchant.................	58.40	17.69	Central Eureka...........	45.2
Calif. Cotton..............	53.08	22.85	El Dorado...............	32.7
Soundview................	40.40	21.37	Blair Holdings...........	29.3
Cons. Chemical...........	36.82	36.93	Golden State.............	25.2
Atlas Imperial............	31.70	20.41	Westates Preferred........	24.9
Di Giorgio................	31.40	8.73	General Paint............	24.3
Golden State..............	30.80	22.90	Pacific Coast Aggregates ...	21.9
General Paint.............	30.06	21.74	Menasco................	20.6
West Pipe................	29.73	12.39	Emporium Capwell.......	20.3
No. Am. Oil..............	23.85	10.58	Western Dept. Stores......	18.7
Hunt Bros................	14.75	6.06	Anglo-Calif. Nat'l Bk......	17.0
Emporium Capwell........	14.60	8.55	S. & W F F..............	15.4
El Dorado................	11.80	2.89	M J M & M..............	14.2
Anglo Calif...............	7.93	7.78	Westates Common........	12.8
Leslie Salt................	7.44	3.69	Dominguez..............	12.5
Hale Bros................	6.96	4.07	Marchant...............	12.1
Magnin, I................	4.86	6.78	Calaveras...............	10.9
Hawaiian Pineapple........	4.54	3.18	Id. Md. Mines............	7.9
Honolulu O. C.............	4.38	4.08	Hawaiian Pineapple.......	6.0

SOURCE: Records of the San Francisco Stock Exchange.

TABLE 17

DISTRIBUTION OF RATIOS OF DAYS-NOT-TRADED TO TOTAL TRADING DAYS
FOR SELECTED SAN FRANCISCO LISTINGS

Years	Number of issues [a]	Percentage ratios of days not traded to total trading days			
		75–100	50–75	25–50	Less than 25
1937.....................	20	5	7	7	1
1938.....................	19 [b]	7	10	1	1
1946.....................	21	1	3	11	6
1953.....................	26	..	5	11	10

SOURCE: Records of the San Francisco Stock Exchange.
[a] Selection of issues is based upon annual trading volume. The issues chosen for 1937 and 1938 are not necessarily the same as those for 1946 and 1953.
[b] Consolidated Chemical omitted.

earnings ratios and yields. Although exhaustive treatment is believed unnecessary, both methods are utilized to demonstrate the presence of substantial market risk. Attention is restricted under the indirect approach to questions of speculative trading and the appropriateness of marketing procedures. Inferences have already been drawn about inadequate volume (in the discussion of salability) and the influence of dominant categories (in the discussion of comparative price patterns).

To round out the previous analysis of dominant security classes, however, one parenthetical remark should perhaps be included at this stage. Data contained in table 18 show that more than half of the issues traded primarily on the San Francisco Exchange belong to four industries. These industries are petroleum, sugar, retail trade, and mining. For the Los Angeles Exchange, petroleum alone has depth.

Earlier conclusions concerning the influence of low-priced stocks notwithstanding, undue concentration of issues among a few industries is likely to augment market risk. Even when the securities market is bullish, investor interest and trading activity exhibit variations among stocks belonging to different industrial groupings. An unbalanced market—under these conditions—may well result in alternations of feast and famine. During periods of famine, specialists on exchanges which feature excessive concentration cannot be expected to perform their functions effectively since the remuneration is low. Nor can member firms whose primary interest lies in profits through trading be expected to evince extraordinary concern over the maintenance of markets for regional listings during inactive periods.

SPECULATIVE TRADING

Information about speculative trading is found in data on security prices and annual share turnover. Although indecisive, price movements in the base sample of leading issues traded primarily on the San Francisco Exchange suggest that speculative activity is relatively limited. Indexes of prices for the sample stocks, exhibited in figure 2, do not reflect—at least for the period 1949 to 1955—the amplitude of fluctuation normally linked with notable variations in speculative interest. Nor has the rise in price of San Francisco listings since 1948 kept pace with the increase in price of New York Exchange issues (as measured by Moody's Index). The relatively large declines in prices experienced by San Francisco

TABLE 18

DISTRIBUTION OF SAN FRANCISCO LISTINGS BY INDUSTRY AND ASSET SIZE FOR 1953
(Dual listings on New York and American Stock exchanges omitted)

Industry	Number of issues	Asset size (in millions of dollars)				
		Under 1	1–10	10–25	25–50	50 and over
Banks (Commercial)	3	..	..	..	..	3
Battery	1	1	..	..	..	..
Cement	5	..	3	2	..	..
Chemical	2	..	1	..	1	..
Equipment (Office)	3	..	2	1	..	..
Furniture	1	..	1	..	..	..
Fruit Growers	4	..	..	3	..	1
Insurance	2	..	..	..	1	1
Mining	6	1	5	..	..	..
Machinery	2	..	2	..	..	..
Petroleum	19	7	9	1	1	1
Salt	1	..	..	1	..	..
Stores (Dep't)	7	..	2	1	4	..
Sugar	9	..	8	1	..	..
Shipping	1	..	..	..	..	1
Telephone	1	..	1	..	..	..
Investment Co.	3	1	1	1	..	..
Transportation	2	..	2	..	..	..
Misc.	2	..	2	..	..	..
Paperboard	1	..	..	..	..	1
Paint	1	..	1	..	..	..
Food Products	1	..	..	1	..	..
Soft Drinks	1	1	..	..	..	..
Syrup	1	..	1	..	..	..
Total	79	11	41	12	7	8

SOURCE: *San Francisco Stock Exchange, 1955,* pp. 11–13.

issues during 1937–1938 and 1946 may of course imply, among other things, the cessation of speculative activity.

Interannum changes in the turnover of San Francisco stocks indicate that speculative trading may be of some importance in individual cases. For the period 1949 to 1955, the average maximum annual turnover of 20 leading San Francisco issues exceeds their average minimum yearly turnover by more than three and one-half times. Sizable variations also occur in share turnover between 1937 and 1938, as shown in table 16.

The lackadaisical movement (1949–1955) in the average prices of leading San Francisco issues appears to be reconcilable with the

TABLE 19

Distribution of Los Angeles Listings by Industry and Asset Size for 1952
(Dual listings on New York, American, and San Francisco exchanges omitted)

Industry	No. of issues	Asset size (millions of dollars)					
		Less than 1	1–10	10–25	25–50	50 and over	No assets listed
Banks (commercial)...............	1	..	..	..	..	1	..
Cement (and other building materials)........................	1	..	1	..	..	..	..
Equipment (office)................	1	..	1	..	..	..	..
Mining..........................	4	..	..	..	..	..	4
Petroleum.......................	10	7	..	..	..	..	3
Miscellaneous [a]....................	2	..	1	..	..	..	1
Food Products...................	2	..	2	..	..	..	..
Total......................	21	7	5	..	..	1	8

Source: Los Angeles Stock Exchange, *Annual Report*, 1954.
[a] Jewelry, motorcycles.

unruly behavior of annual turnover ratios. Peak turnover ratios for the sample issues are well dispersed throughout the six-year period, with the exception of 1954. In 1954, seven peak ratios are attained, as opposed to two or three in each of the preceding years. The implication may well be that speculative attention ordinarily directs itself to specific issues which change from time to time, but rarely at the regional market as a whole. Since indexes of average prices for groups of stocks present composite pictures, group behavior is likely to be substantially more stable than that of individual issues.

The issue of speculative trading is left somewhat in doubt. Extended analysis requires recurrent surveys to determine the motives underlying buy or sell orders.[23] Indexes of speculative activity (based upon the number of traders interested in short-term appreciation)

[23] Surveys of this nature are periodically undertaken by the New York Stock Exchange, but not by regional exchanges.

could be prepared from these surveys and correlated with fluctuations in security prices.

MEDIA AND MARKETING PROCEDURES

In reviewing the suitability of marketing procedures employed by regional exchanges at least three points deserve consideration. The first concerns the size and distribution by industry of the corporations whose stocks are listed on regional exchanges. Information of this type, when supplemented by data on security prices, yields, and price-earnings ratios, indicates the nature of the media traded. The second pertains to the propriety of regional exchange techniques in the light of the issues traded. The third item relates to the implicit assumption that the present listings on regional exchanges represent those issues which are best suited for regional trading.

Here as well as elsewhere, illustrative material is drawn principally from the San Francisco and Los Angeles exchanges. Table 18 shows the distribution of San Francisco listings (common stocks) by industry and by asset size of issuing corporations for 1953, and table 19 exhibits similar data for the Los Angeles Exchange. Issues dually traded on the New York or American exchanges are omitted.

The significant feature of regional listings for present purposes is their relatively small size. A substantial majority of all companies whose shares are traded primarily on the San Francisco and Los Angeles exchanges had total assets amounting to less than $10,-000,000 at the end of 1953. More than one-third possessed less than $5,000,000 of assets.

These statistics seem to conflict with the initially espoused ideas as to the kind of corporations whose shares may properly be listed. So far as asset size is indicative, the criterion that the listing company be well-known throughout the trading area of the exchange fails to be satisfied by a sizable proportion of regional listings. Share turnover and other data reveal further that regional listings, in many instances, do not meet the second criterion of widely distributed shares.

The consequence is that exchange procedures are imperfectly adapted to the requirements of regional listings as presently constituted. Final judgment concerning the suitability of marketing techniques utilized by regional exchanges must await examination of the over-the-counter area. The apparent success of this division of the securities market suggests that analysis of its features offers excellent opportunities for isolating deficiencies in regional exchanges. Suffice it to say for the moment that less-than-ideal trading arrangements apparently contribute to the market risk featured by regional exchanges.

Confinement of attention to issues now listed regionally places regional exchanges in an unfortunate light. Numerous over-the-counter stocks are undoubtedly better suited to regional exchange procedures. The market risk for these securities (assuming they were listed) is presumably lower than that for many currently listed securities.

Investment services and *Statistics of Income* furnish clues as to the number of firms qualified to list their shares regionally. Moody's Investment Service reports regularly on some 13,500 industrials, utilities, transportation companies, banks, and insurance companies. Standard and Poor's publishes information on 3,922 corporations traded over-the-counter, as compared with 1,326 by Fitch Investors Service. Data contained in *Statistics of Income* reveal that the proportion of listed to total companies with assets ranging between $5,000,000 and $50,000,000 may be as low as 10 per cent.[24]

In spite of the large number of over-the-counter firms whose shares are characterized by reasonable activity, original listings with regional exchanges are distressingly few. The paucity of new listings implies that stocks traded primarily on regional exchanges tend to be increasingly restricted to those in which the issuing company has failed to develop to the point where national listing is desirable. When associated with reluctance on the part of regional exchanges to take delisting action, the result is likely to be that regional listings are far from ideal.

PRICE-EARNINGS RATIOS AND YIELDS

The matter of market risk can be approached directly through the medium of historical multipliers (i.e., price-earnings ratios) and yields. Utilization of these relationships, as opposed to indexes of security prices, permits partial elimination of the effects of earnings and dividend variations upon stock prices. The amplitude and frequency of fluctuations in price-earnings ratios and yields thus reflect the degree of risk involved better than do most measures.[25]

---

[24] See, for example, *Statistics of Income for 1951*, Part II, p. 126.

[25] The principal defect of historical multipliers and yields is that, since they deal with past events, full account cannot be taken of *expected future changes* in earnings and dividends.

TABLE 20

Price-Earnings Ratios and Yields for Twenty-Three San Francisco Listings During the Period 1949–1954

Listing company[a]	Ratios of price to earnings in per cent					Ratios of dividends to price in per cent				
	1953	1952	1951	1950	1949	1949	1950	1951	1952	1953
Intex Oil	17.8X	20.2X	20.6X	22.9X	20.7X	0	0	0	0	0
General Paint	17.3	18.7	4.8	4.1	8.8	1.1	8.5	7.5	6.4	0
Oceanic Oil	14.8	37.0	962.5	31.7	26.6	0	0	0	0	0
Blair Holdings	11.9	9.7	b	18.1	8.7	4.4	5.5	4.3	0	5.2
Matson	11.3	9.4	8.9	7.9	b	0	6.5	6.0	6.7	8.6
Douglas Oil	11.0	...	...	...	...	...	...	...	...	1.7
Anglo-Calif.	10.1	9.9	10.1	8.4	8.9	4.9	4.3	5.5	5.2	4.8
Dominguez Oil	9.2	9.6	9.5	8.3	6.2	13.9	12.3	10.6	9.3	9.4
Pac. Coast Agg.	8.6	7.7	5.2	4.8	10.5	6.8	7.4	10.3	9.7	8.5
Marchant	7.8	7.5	6.8	3.9	4.1	10.1	11.2	9.4	7.6	7.8
Golden State	7.4	7.1	9.8	9.4	7.6	8.0	7.2	7.1	6.6	5.4
S. & W. F. F.	6.9	b	4.9	7.2	...	6.4	7.2	7.7	0	0
Emporium Capwell	6.7	7.2	8.8	5.5	4.9	11.1	9.5	7.2	5.9	7.2
Hawaiian Pineapple	6.3	12.1	7.2	5.3	5.8	9.7	10.6	6.1	0	4.5
Menasco	6.3	6.5	8.5	26.4	6.7	0	0	0	6.3	7.3
West Dep't Store	6.1	6.0	4.9	4.5	3.9	10.2	8.8	7.3	8.7	8.5
Calaveras	5.2	29.5	9.1	4.4	1.3	0	1.7	6.3	1.8	4.0
Morr-Knudson	5.6	6.0	5.0	4.1	2.9	6.6	8.2	5.2	4.8	7.2
M. J. M. & M.	b	b	b	113.7	49.4	5.1	4.4	1.3	0	0
El Dorado	b	b	b	7.0	21.6	12.0	11.7	9.5	0	0
Central Eureka	b	b	b	19.2	b	...	...	...	...	...
Westates	b	b	b	b	b	0	0	0	0	0
Id-Md.	b	b	b	b	b	0	0	0	0	0

SOURCE: Records of the San Francisco Stock Exchange.
[a] Arranged in order of 1953 price-earnings ratios.
b Deficit.

TABLE 21

PRICE-EARNINGS RATIOS AND YIELDS FOR SELECTED SAN FRANCISCO LISTINGS

Listing company	1946 Price-earnings ratio	1946 Yield	Listing company	1938 Price-earnings ratio	1938 Yield	1937 Price-earnings ratio	1937 Yield
M. J. M. & M.	72.5X	.03	Union Sugar	27.0X	1.1	a	0
Blair Holdings	60.3	2.6	Honolulu Oil	19.1	4.1	19.7X	5.0
Pac. Coast Agg.	44.6	6.6	Anglo-Calif.	16.8	3.0	11.9	4.2
Matson	25.8	3.8	Leslie Salt	14.1	6.6	14.9	7.0
Hawaiian Pineapple	17.9	4.7	Atlas	14.0	0	20.7	0
Menasco	15.5	0	Soundview	13.2	8.8	67.3	0
Dominguez	10.4	9.5	Cons. Chemical	10.9	5.5	41.0	8.7
Golden State	10.3	3.6	Hawaiian Pineapple	10.7	7.2	14.4	12.3
Anglo-Calif.	7.5	3.3	El Dorado	10.4	7.9	a	8.6
Intex Oil	7.5	0	Magnin, I.	9.9	6.5	11.9	8.3
El Dorado	7.4	10.2	No. Amer. Oil	9.8	7.6	13.2	8.5
West Dep't Stores	5.7	4.8	West. Pipe & Steel	9.4	11.0	34.2	5.0
S. & W. F. F.	5.3	6.0	Hale Bros.	6.6	12.7	12.7	7.3
Marchant	4.8	5.5	Emporium Capwell	6.4	8.3	7.3	9.8
Emporium Capwell	4.7	6.2	General Paint	6.3	4.3	23.4	5.9
General Paint	4.6	3.8	Marchant	5.6	15.2	7.8	9.0
Central Eureka	a	0	Di Giorgio	a	0	a	0
Calaveras	a	0	Golden State	a	0	a	0
Id.-Md.	a	0	Hunt Bros.	a	14.7	a	0
Westates	a	0	Calif. Cotton	a	0	a	0

SOURCE: Records of the San Francisco Stock Exchange.
a Deficit or near deficit.

Although absolute standards cannot be readily established, comparisons are possible between the multipliers and yields for regional listings and those for national listings.[26] The greater the similarity of their behavior over time and the more nearly equal the multipliers and yields (for issues of equivalent risk), the smaller is the divergence of market risk associated with regional exchanges from that attached to national exchanges.

Tables 20 and 21 record historical price-earnings ratios and yields, during the periods 1937–1939, 1946, and 1949–1954, for volume leaders traded primarily on the San Francisco Exchange. The most noticeable feature of these data is their dispersion. If firms which consistently incur deficits are omitted, peak multipliers are, for example, evenly spread throughout the period 1949–1954.

Only 3 regional issues exhibit exactly the same pattern from 1950 to 1954 as that shown by leading industrial securities. The principal similarity between national and regional listings during this period occurs in 1950. In that year, minimum multipliers (1949 excluded) were achieved by 10 of the 23 regional issues.

Extreme dispersion in the multipliers and yields shown in table 20 precludes definitive statements about relative levels. Several of the San Francisco volume leaders appear to be largely speculative in nature and cannot be used for comparative purposes. For the higher quality regional listings, however, multipliers tend to be somewhat lower and/or yields higher than those for leading industrials. This differential is consistent with the proposition that market risk is believed by investors to be greater for regional exchanges than for national exchanges.

Changes between 1946 and 1949–1954 evince an absence of uniformity similar to the 1949–1954 period. In six instances, where comparisons are possible, ratios of price to earnings for 1946 are below those for 1949–1954; in seven instances, the reverse obtains. Only in the years 1937–1939 does a likeness of pattern exist. For the issues shown in table 21, price-earnings ratios for 1937 generally exceed those for 1938.

Failure on the part of these securities to behave alike confirms

[26] Price-earnings ratios and yields for 125 leading industrial securities, as provided by Standard and Poor's, are as follows:

Year	Price-earnings ratio	Yield in per cent
1953	9.9	5.51
1952	10.6	5.55
1951	9.6	6.29
1950	6.8	6.51

our opinion as to the heterogeneity of stocks traded on the San Francisco Exchange. It suggests that the risk attached to the assets in question may be of greater consequence than market risk. Additional justification for this conclusion is found in the relatively small size and uncertain prospects of many regional corporations.

Although interesting, further analysis of historical price-earnings ratios and yields does not seem worthwhile. The point is amply demonstrated that few regional issues are characterized by great stability. Limitations inherent in historical ratios prevent, however, precise measurement of the degree of market risk.

CONCLUSIONS

To conclude, serious doubts exist as to the effectiveness of regional exchanges (as represented by the San Francisco Exchange) in carrying out their basic function of providing satisfactory liquidity to regional issues. Salability, as reflected in trading activity, trading continuity, and ratios of individual to total transactions, is mediocre. Market risk, as reflected in the diversity of issue quality, the lack of balanced listings, the inability to obtain new listings, the variability of price-earnings ratios and of yields, and other considerations underlying salability, is considerable.

Of prime significance is the desirability of obtaining new listings which possess reasonable quality. For suggestions both as to needed improvements in trading procedures and as to methods of encouraging additional listings, we turn now to a consideration of over-the-counter trading.

V

Over-the-Counter Trading: A Major Source of Competition for Regional Security Exchanges

The foregoing analysis of the performance of regional exchanges reveals, among other things, two facts of special relevance to this chapter. One is the substantial reliance upon multiple trading in nationally listed stocks by regional exchanges. The other and related item is the apparent success achieved by the over-the-counter segment in capturing and holding the stocks of medium-size, regional corporations.

Heavy reliance upon multiply traded securities reflects a failure by regional exchanges to attain independence status. Given their limited contributions to the market depth of multiple listings, regional exchanges must look elsewhere to justify their existence. Elsewhere, in this instance, appears to be the attraction and satisfactory servicing of good quality, but currently unlisted, securities. Encroachment upon over-the-counter preserves is, however, more easily said than accomplished.

The evidence at hand indicates that regional exchanges are currently little more than poor relations to their over-the-counter counterparts. At least two corporations have requested (and received) in recent months stockholder permission to withdraw their common stock from listing on regional exchanges. Morrison-Knudsen removed its shares from listing on the San Francisco Exchange, and Maine Central Railroad delisted its stock from the Boston Exchange.

In both instances, the opinion is expressed that over-the-counter dealers can provide improved markets. According to the proxy statement of Maine Central Railroad, dated February 23, 1955:

Management believes that the existence of this [the Boston Stock] Exchange market for this stock, with its relatively infrequent transactions, has been detrimental to the company by discouraging dealers in the over-the-counter market, particularly those in Maine, from making a market for the stock. In this connection, it may be noted that the number of stockholders in Maine has decreased from 1,128 in 1931 to 299 in December 1954, while the total number of stockholders has decreased from 1,617 to 717 in the same period. . . . The Management believes that the result of withdrawal from listing would tend to increase the interest by over-the-counter dealers in the stock and thus provide the stock with a better and broader market. . . .

In a similar vein, the management of Morrison-Knudsen, in a proxy statement dated May 8, 1954, argues that the absence of substantial activity on the San Francisco Exchange "acts as a deterrent to interest by securities brokers and dealers in the corporation's stock." The point is made that share turnover in 1953 was only 3 per cent and that more than two-thirds of the transactions were originated by one firm, Wegener and Daly of Boise, Idaho. The conclusion is that shareholdings have tended to become increasingly localized and that delisting is essential to counteract this unfortunate circumstance.

SURVEY OF LISTED AND UNLISTED CORPORATIONS

If the attitudes expressed by the managements of these 2 companies are at all prevalent, it behooves us to ascertain the factors which underlie over-the-counter achievements. In order to confirm or deny these opinions and to gain insight into those benefits peculiar to over-the-counter trading, reference is made to data derived from a survey of 22 corporations whose shares are traded over-the-counter. The points raised in the responses from the sample companies are then divided into three categories for further analysis. The basis for segregation is whether the reasons for not listing pertain to trading procedures, variations in the degree of regulation, or other considerations.

UNLISTED COMPANIES

The sample of 22 over-the-counter corporations is selected from a group of firms deemed suitable by Ronald E. Kaehler for listing on the San Francisco Stock Exchange. The president of each com-

TABLE 22

REASONS SPECIFIED BY 19 OVER-THE-COUNTER COMPANIES FOR CHOOSING NOT TO LIST THEIR SECURITIES, BROKEN DOWN BY INDUSTRY

	No. of firms	No appar. advan.	Loss of dealer interest	Reporting requirements		Need more seasoning	Lack available sponsorship	Securities closely held	Avoiding speculation	Not qualified
				Too onerous	No prob.					
Agricultural products	1	…	1	…	1	…	1	…	…	…
Baby foods	1	…	1	…	1	…	…	…	…	…
Cement	1	…	1	…	1	…	…	…	1	…
Dairy prod.	2	…	1	2	…	…	…	1	1	…
Elect. power	2	2	1	1	…	…	…	…	…	…
Gas transmission	2	2	…	…	2	…	…	…	…	…
Machinery parts, tools and equip.	4	…	3	…	2	2	…	1	…	…
Petroleum	1	…	…	…	…	…	…	…	…	1
Plywood	1	…	…	1	…	1	…	…	…	…
Radio and TV	2	1	1	…	…	1	…	…	1	…
Retail trade	2	1	2	…	…	1	…	1	…	…
Total	19	6	11	4	7	4	1	3	3	1

SOURCE: Written responses to questionnaire.

pany was asked by letter to indicate why his firm chose not to list its securities. Responses exceeded 95 per cent.[1]

A tabulation of the survey results, broken down by industry, is presented in table 22. In view of the limited size of the sample, the reasons recorded in table 22 may or may not be representative.

One consideration evoking widespread attention, in addition to the diverse other factors to which less frequent reference is made, emerges from the survey of companies whose issues are traded over-the-counter. More than half of the answering companies evince concern over the possible loss of dealer interest which might result from listing their issues. Five stress specifically the desirability of higher broker profits to encourage augmented selling effort. Implicit in several statements is an attitude of uncertainty as to whether the present satisfactory market for the stock would be maintained after listing. Only one respondent avers that arguments put forth by security dealers pertaining to loss of interest should not be taken too seriously.

With the possible exception of 3 closely held corporations, virtually all those surveyed are technically qualified for listing.[2] Several nevertheless indicate a need for further seasoning before listing. Of these companies, 5 express an ultimate interest in listing. The opinion seems to be generally held that the initial task of distributing stock among large numbers of investors and over wide geographic areas can be achieved more effectively by over-the-counter dealers. Here, as in dealer interest, the question of adequate incentive arises.

A sizable proportion of the sample firms takes the position that no appreciable benefits accrue from listing. The vice-president of one corporation states that "too much emphasis is placed upon the advantages of listing securities. In all instances . . . the off-board activities . . . determine the market acceptance of any security." To the extent that this opinion prevails, factors, such as reporting requirements and registration expense which would otherwise be inconsequential, assume a degree of importance.

Both the preceding point and the one relating to the uncertainty which encompasses the effects of listing suggest a fundamental competitive advantage of the over-the-counter segment. This advantage

---

[1] Of the 21 responses, one is not usable. In addition, two companies in the process of merging answered as a single corporation.

[2] The sole other exception is a petroleum producer in the exploratory stage of development. Since this company is still capitalizing exploration expenses, it is unable to prepare a profit and loss statement.

arises from the fact that all issues are initially traded over-the-counter and that new issues, whether or not the company has listed its outstanding securities, are distributed over-the-counter. Over-the-counter dealers are thus able to impress their point of view upon corporations much earlier than the organized exchanges and to exert a continuing influence through their investment banking functions.

Recognition as the primary market for an unlisted issue affords certain monopolistic privileges to over-the-counter dealers. As the issuer of a given security achieves success over time, the value of these privileges increases. At the very time when stocks become eligible for listing with organized exchanges, therefore, dealer resistance to such a change is likely to be at its peak.

Under these circumstances, listing may well be deferred until the advantages are overwhelming.[3] The choice is not simply one of two alternatives; it involves direct action by the unlisted firm in the face of dealer opposition. It also involves a comparison of *known* over-the-counter performance with *unknown* behavior on the organized exchanges.

Mention should be made of at least two further considerations raised by certain of the respondents. One pertains to the wish expressed by a few companies to avoid speculative activity in their issues. The opinion is advanced that over-the-counter trading is more conducive both to permanent security holders and to short-term price stability than is trading on organized exchanges. A similar position is also taken by many leading financial institutions. If less speculation does indeed occur in the over-the-counter area, it presumably results from the absence of publicity concerning over-the-counter transactions.

The other item relates to the prestige, or lack thereof, associated with regional exchanges. The president of one corporation goes so far as to say that any intermediate step between over-the-counter trading and listing on the New York Stock Exchange represents little more than a compromise. Prestige is undoubtedly a vital consideration so far as the future success of regional exchanges is concerned. Because of its significance and its relevance to questions relating to mergers among regional exchanges, treatment of exchange status is reserved for special attention in the chapter on mergers.

---

[3] For many corporations, this situation, moreover, may never exist.

Listed Companies

A similar survey was conducted of 23 regional corporations whose securities are among the volume leaders on the San Francisco Exchange.[4] The president of each company was asked to indicate, among other things, the purposes underlying the initial listing of the stock, the benefits which had accrued from listing, and possible improvements in the procedures of the San Francisco Exchange. Fifteen usable responses were received.

The results of this survey are introduced at this point for two reasons. First, the opinions expressed may reveal whether or not the executives of corporations whose shares are traded over-the-counter are unduly influenced by the attitudes of over-the-counter dealers. Second, additional clues may be provided as to the degree of competition between regional exchanges and the over-the-counter segment.

Although various listing objectives are specified, emphasis is placed upon broader distribution of shares and increased marketability (as reflected in greater activity). In three instances, listing is reported to have been associated with the public sale of securities. In two cases, the immediate need was to create a satisfactory market for the shares of stockholders wishing to dispose of their holdings. The avowed purpose of one firm was to increase the distribution of stock in the Northwest areas where a substantial part of its business is done.

Other factors mentioned include the effect of listing upon the ability to use stock as collateral for loans, the prestige and good will in the financial and business community, the participation of many—as opposed to a few—brokerage firms, and the ownership affiliation with member firms. The latter item is sufficiently interesting to elaborate. The controlling interest of one company is stated to have been associated at the time of listing (1938) with a member firm of the New York Stock Exchange which was not a member of the San Francisco Exchange. Since the reciprocity ratio for New York firms at that time was estimated to be $2 or $3 in commissions for every dollar generated for San Francisco firms, pressure from this source was exerted for listing.

As the preceding remarks suggest, the purposes which underlie listing are sometimes associated with other considerations than

---

[4] The securities of these firms are included in the base-sample used to prepare the price index for the San Francisco Exchange.

improving the position of shareholders as a group and reducing financing costs. To illustrate this point further, a commercial bank executive indicates that his institution listed its issues at a time before the passage of legislation restricting the investment banking activities of commercial banks. The initial reason for listing was apparently to promote investment banking business and to obtain additional deposits from the financial community.

Since the majority of the firms surveyed are truly regional in nature, only scattered reference is made in the responses to the basis for selecting the San Francisco Exchange, in preference to other exchanges. Wherever sizable corporations which qualify for listing on the national exchanges confine themselves to the San Francisco Exchange, the determining factor appears, as a rule, to be concentrated shareholdings. Officials of 3 companies specifically stress this consideration.[5] One firm in this category went so far as to list its stock on the New York Stock Exchange, but delisted when activity thereon failed to meet expectations.

Among the benefits actually obtained from listing, the majority of respondents indicate that marketability has improved and distribution of shares has become more widespread. In two cases, however, doubts are raised as to whether listing had greatly augmented activity. In one case, the point is made that listing probably caused the number of shareholders to decrease.

As a partial check of opinions about marketability and distribution, questions were posed as to the influence of listing upon the cost of new issues. Unfortunately, few of the corporations surveyed have experience upon which to draw. Only in two responses is the belief expressed and supported by evidence that the terms of new issues are improved through listing.

The president of a small oil exploration company indicates that the broadened distribution of shareholdings occasioned by listing facilitates new financing through the utilization of preëmptive rights. The point is made that small firms cannot readily afford to distribute new issues by means of the investment banking process. Their best source of funds therefore becomes existing stockholders. In the oil company in question, three successful distributions have been made directly to shareholders in recent years, and a further one is under consideration.

Three additional advantages realized from listing with regional exchanges are also mentioned. Two answers refer directly (and

---

[5] In each instance, it is interesting to note, their observations are supported by the behavior of annual share turnover ratios.

others indirectly) to the benefits of daily publicity. One attaches significance to the convenience of dealing with brokers locally. Two others stress the opportunity obtained through listing to become acquainted with individuals and firms in the investment banking business.

Approximately half of the responses contain no recommendations for improving the operations and procedures of the San Francisco Exchange. The remainder provide a wide variety of suggestions. In one instance, it is stated that "almost anything would be an improvement." Less extreme proposals include revision of commission schedules, more frequent plant visits by the exchange members, increased efforts to acquaint investors with the policies of firms in which they invest, and monthly reports to "listed" companies showing the distribution of security purchases by area. The corporation executive commenting on changes in commission schedules is concerned with the present discrimination against low-priced issues.[6] This point may be of considerable significance since low-priced issues often constitute the bulk of stocks traded primarily on regional exchanges.

Although the replies are for the most part favorable, no definite conclusions can be drawn from the survey of listed corporations. The reason is simply that listing by these firms took place in most cases some time before World War II. Broadened distribution and augmented trading activity may have been connected with such factors as growth and increased profitability, as well as with listing. In addition, substantial progress has been made over the past two decades in the servicing of over-the-counter securities, whereas the status of regional exchanges has tended to deteriorate. An indisputable fact is that medium-size corporations—whether for real or imagined reasons—have not listed their securities in appreciable quantities.

If the proposition is accepted for purposes of analysis that over-the-counter markets possess certain competitive advantages, the problem becomes one of examining underlying causes and of determining whether they are inherent in the over-the-counter type of distribution channel. To accomplish this task, let us consider—in the order listed—the effects of variations in government regulation, of differences in distribution procedures, and of other factors.

---

[6] The commission on multiples of 100 shares is determined by multiplying the 100-share rate by the number of 100's involved. As a result, a given dollar purchase of a low-priced issue involves a higher commission (in excess of 100 shares) than the same dollar amount invested in high-priced issues.

REGULATION OF OVER-THE-COUNTER ISSUES

The point has already been made that federal regulation distinguishes between listed and unlisted securities. Section 12 of the Securities Exchange Act specifies that continuation of registration on organized exchanges is dependent upon filing with the Securities and Exchange Commission current reports in the event of material changes and annual reports within one hundred and twenty days (unless extended) subsequent to the termination of the fiscal year. Section 16 of the same Act requires each officer and beneficial owner of more than 10 per cent of any type of registered equity security to file initial reports of his holdings and monthly reports of changes therein. The Securities and Exchange Commission publishes monthly summaries of these reports, and speculative profits based upon inside information may be recovered by the corporation or by any security holder in its behalf. The Securities and Exchange Commission, through its regulations, further prescribes that proxies must contain sufficient information to permit intelligent action by the shareholders.

No such requirements exist for the issuers of unlisted securities. Regulation in the over-the-counter segment of the securities market is restricted largely to self-government, and stresses ethical behavior by the security dealers.[7] Under Section 15 of the Exchange Act, as amended in 1936, the Securities and Exchange Commission is simply given very general power to control fraudulent conduct in the over-the-counter area.

The situation fortunately is not as bad as the preceding comments indicate. Any unexempted corporation contemplating a new security issue which aggregates $300,000 or more must submit a registration statement to the Securities and Exchange Commission and must prepare a prospectus for distribution. Unlisted companies may be asked to make public from time to time detailed information of the same type as is periodically provided by listed firms. The president of one unlisted firm states:

We filed with the Securities and Exchange Commission at the time of our merger with . . . and we are keeping our accounting substantially in conformity with S.E.C. reporting requirements, although of course we do not actually file the reports other than those which are required.

---

[7] H. C. Westwood and E. C. Howard, "Self-Government in the Securities Business," *Law and Contemporary Problems* (Duke University School of Law, Durham, N.C., Summer, 1952), pp. 518–544.

It would be no particular additional trouble to comply with the registration and reporting requirements.

As revealed in table 22, the attitudes of over-the-counter corporations toward the reporting requirements of listed companies are mixed. A majority of the firms whose issues have excellent trading potential on organized exchanges probably does not regard the additional paper work as unduly burdensome. The fact that a sizable number of corporations does view the reporting requirements associated with listing as onerous is, however, of considerable relevance.

The position taken herein is that governmental regulation of securities should not discriminate among marketing channels. To the extent that differences in reporting requirements discourage firms from listing their issues, the distribution of issues between channels is arbitrarily distorted. Unless it can be said that one form is (somehow) socially preferable to the other, artificial barriers of this type cannot be justified.

If adequate reporting by corporations is desirable, the solution appears to lie in changing the basis for filing reports. A reasonable alternative to the listing criterion might well be asset-size. In addition to being relatively neutral as far as marketing channels are concerned, this criterion—or some other similar one—permits limitation in the number of affected companies to an amount which is administratively feasible for the Securities and Exchange Commission.

From time to time, legislation has been introduced to achieve this end. A current bill (S. 2054) sponsored by Senator Fulbright, would subject, as originally drafted, to provisions of the Securities and Exchange Act all corporations having assets of $5,000,000 or more and shareholders numbering 500 or more. In testimony before a Senate Banking Subcommittee, G. Keith Funston, president of the New York Stock Exchange, advocated reduction of the standard to $3,000,000 of assets and 300 shareholders.[8] The "$5,000,000–500" criteria cover, in his opinion, about 1,300 unlisted companies; the "$3,000,000–300" criteria, approximately 1,800 over-the-counter corporations. Although only 120 of these corporations satisfy the $7,000,000 asset requirement of the New York Stock Exchange, many are purported to be eligible for listing their securities on regional exchanges.

---

[8] *Wall Street Journal* (Pacific Coast edition), July 1, 1955.

Revisions in S. 2054, as approved by a Senate Banking Subcommittee, impose Securities and Exchange Commission rules upon unlisted companies having 750 or more shareholders in any single class of securities or bonds registered with the Commission, whose principal amount equals or exceeds $1,000,000.[9] Despite the recommendation of the Securities and Exchange Commission that there be no assets test, the amended bill provides for the exemption of corporations whose assets are less than $2,000,000. Registration automatically becomes unnecessary whenever assets decline below $1,000,000, shareholders number less than 500, and outstanding debt is reduced below $1,000,000. Application for exemption can be made wherever issues are characterized by inactive trading and little public interest. To the list of organizations normally exempt from Securities and Exchange regulations are added insurance companies.

OVER-THE-COUNTER PROCEDURES

Elimination of double standards assumes importance to regional exchanges only if the advantages provided by listing exceed those derived from over-the-counter trading. Of perhaps greater significance in governing the choice between listing and not listing, therefore, are the distribution procedures of the over-the-counter segment. Brokerage firms are, as indicated earlier, the primary markets for securities traded over-the-counter. The unique features of this division of the securities market are restricted publicity, variable commissions (or spreads), dealers acting as principals, and salesmen associated directly with the primary markets.

EFFECT OF LIMITED PUBLICITY

By "restricted publicity" is meant that information pertaining to the volume of transactions in individual over-the-counter issues is not made available to the public.[10] Public reporting is limited largely to nominal "bid" and "asked" quotations compiled by the National Quotation Bureau. As implied by the term "nominal," these quotations need not reflect the exact prices at which unlisted shares are bought and sold.

The effect of secrecy is to render the market for over-the-counter

---

[9] *Ibid.*, "Bill Backed Applying SEC Rules to Certain Unlisted Companies," July 30, 1955.

[10] Studies conducted at the University of Pennsylvania and sponsored by the Merrill Foundation shed light upon the total volume of over-the-counter transactions, but detailed periodic information remains unavailable.

securities somewhat less than perfect. Bid and offered prices for a given stock are uniform neither among brokerage firms even within the same trading area nor among customers. Nor are the demand and supply conditions for over-the-counter issues known with any degree of certainty.

The justification for restricted publicity, if there is one, revolves around the reactions of security traders. There is reason to believe that short-term holders often base their decisions to buy or to sell stocks upon price and volume movements.[11] To the extent that such is the case, secrecy may well curtail speculative activity.

A similar type of argument is employed in connection with the purchase or sale of large blocks of securities by financial institutions. If publicized, large transactions might induce chain reactions. For the cumulative effect to be significant, the presumption must of course be that transactions of this nature reflect informed opinion as to the over or under valuation of the securities in question.

Evidence that speculation in over-the-counter stocks is limited is reported to be found in the behavior of over-the-counter prices. That is to say, day-to-day variations in unlisted issues are frequently believed to be smaller than those in listed securities. The president of one over-the-counter company which has more than 8,000 shareholders states that: "It is our observation that price swings of our stock have been less marked under the present system. There seems to be somewhat of an insulation from day to day developments on the stock exchange which are probably responsible for having brought about this result."

Since continuous records of prices at which over-the-counter orders are executed do not exist, the preceding point can neither be proven nor disproven. It is nonetheless demonstrable that the over-the-counter segment is not immune from speculative activity. To show this point, we have only to refer to the interest exhibited by brokerage firms in speculative trading media. The July 2, 1954, issue of *The National Monthly Stock Summary,* published by the National Quotation Bureau, reveals, for example, 59 dealers interested in U. S. Thermo Control during the period April 1, 1954, to July 1, 1954, 54 in Haile Mines, 53 in Colorado Oil and Gas, 45 in Pubco Development, and 43 in Magnolia Parks.[12]

[11] See, for example, "The Biggest Stock Market in America," *Commercial and Financial Chronicle,* April 8, 1954.

[12] The choice of issues is based primarily upon their price and upon the business of the issuer.

The conclusion might well be drawn that distinction should be made among classes of speculative activity. It is reasonable to suppose that day-to-day trading by chartists and technical traders in over-the-counter issues is limited. If such were not the case, a necessary assumption would be that price and volume changes in the over-the-counter segment parallel those in the organized exchanges. It is equally legitimate to presume that recommendations and "tips" by security salesmen are important in over-the-counter trading. If this presumption is valid, speculation of a different sort is likely to be encouraged.

At any rate, restricted publicity permits price discrimination and enables over-the-counter dealers to harvest monopoly profits. It therefore encourages the firms in question to urge strongly against listing.

Without pursuing the matter further, let us accept the proposition that over-the-counter trading is not conducive to certain types of speculative activity. Let us agree, as seems reasonable, that the prime factor producing this result is limited publicity.[13] Let us further agree that, though excessive speculation is undesirable, a certain amount is needed to achieve an adequate volume of trading. The question then arises as to how organized exchanges may, on the one hand, best counteract the argument that they are characterized by undue speculation and, on the other, reduce the opposition of broker firms to the listing of additional issues.

One possibility is to urge the passage of legislation requiring the periodic disclosure of over-the-counter trading activity and of actual prices at which orders are executed. The matter of dual standards arises at this juncture in much the same fashion as it does in connection with corporate reporting requirements. If it is deemed socially desirable to make public price and volume data for listed securities, the same would seem to hold for over-the-counter issues.

The resultant reduction of market imperfections and curtailment of opportunities for monopoly profits in unlisted, that is, over-the-counter trading, can be expected to decrease the opposition of over-the-counter dealers to the listing of qualified stocks. A necessary assumption is of course that the more important over-

---

[13] A secondary factor is that over-the-counter issues cannot be purchased on the margin, although they can be employed as collateral for loans. Since the margin requirement has been 50 per cent or more for most of the postwar period, this consideration is presumed to have less force than that of restricted publicity.

the-counter traders are either exchange members or have ready access to exchange privileges. Disadvantages of public reporting, such as augmented speculative activity, may—if they are truly significant—be handled by direct action.

Public reporting of price and transactions data for unlisted stocks need not impose undue burdens upon either security dealers or collecting agencies. Administrative difficulties can be limited by confining the reporting firms to the larger over-the-counter traders and by prescribing minimum size and number of shareholders criteria for corporations whose issues are required to have public disclosure of prices and volume. The utilization of asset-size or similar standards further reduces the likelihood of discrimination between organized exchanges and the over-the-counter division.

In the event legislation is not feasible (or even if it is), a second possibility merits attention. Organized exchanges themselves can take steps to eliminate the less desirable aspects of speculation. For example, exchanges might alter the system of brokerage commissions in order to reduce the incentive for active trading. That part of the latest revision (November 9, 1953) in the minimum commission schedule which authorizes lower rates where stocks turn over in less than thirty days could well be abandoned on this basis. The relation of charges to service costs, rather than to individual transactions is also worthy of consideration. A special committee of the American Stock Exchange has in fact already recommended that fees be charged for services which are currently free.[14]

Again, exchanges might reëxamine their educational programs. The less fortunate features of speculation appear to thrive on investor misconceptions. There is reason to believe that speculative activity ceases to be a major problem when investors become qualified to judge the value of "tips" and to interpret correctly the basis for market behavior.

Whether those associated with organized exchanges actually benefit from changes designed to lessen speculative trading depends upon the relative importance of offsetting influences. Reduced speculation decreases the transactions volume in individual issues; whereas additions to listings attributable to this factor raise aggregate activity. The initial effect is likely to be a diminution in total

[14] "American Exchange Group Suggests Rates for Some Services Now Free," *Wall Street Journal* (Pacific Coast edition), July 9, 1954. It should be pointed out that this group did not concern itself with the avoidance of speculation.

trading on the organized exchange(s) with a gradually rising volume if, and when, additional issues are induced by the reduction in speculative activity to list.

Of some relevance to the West Coast exchanges (and perhaps to regional exchanges in general) is the fact that some corporations list their stock in the hope that speculative interest will be created.[15] Young, growing companies often acknowledge the desirability of speculative activity in order to facilitate the issuance of new shares at attractive prices. A primary source of new listings for the San Francisco and Los Angeles exchanges has been petroleum exploration and production ventures. If speculative activity were diminished appreciably, it is doubtful whether such firms would care to list their issues.

Day-to-day fluctuations in the prices of issues traded principally on regional exchanges appear to be smaller than short-term movements in the prices of national listings. This conclusion is drawn from an observation of daily price movements in issues traded on the San Francisco Exchange for the period October 14, 1954, to March 31, 1955. It is supported by the fact that commercial banks, which as a group are sensitive about publicized variations in the prices of their shares, are relatively more willing to have their issues listed on regional exchanges than on the national exchanges.[16] In addition to those listed on the San Francisco Exchange, the stocks of twelve Washington banks are traded on the Philadelphia–Baltimore Exchange.

Questions of speculative activity may, as a consequence, not greatly deter corporations from listing their issues on regional exchanges. Such considerations may apply primarily to listing on national exchanges. Regional exchanges should perhaps be more concerned with matters of prestige and marketing procedures.

As a parenthetical note, it should be mentioned that speculation, if reasonable, serves a definite purpose. Speculative trading broadens the market and stabilizes prices through time, provided the pressures exerted are not cumulative in one direction. Its danger is that excessive fluctuations in security prices are encouraged by the appearance and disappearance of unskilled speculators. The organized segment of the securities market is extremely susceptible to the latter.

---

[15] In accordance with our earlier discussion, it may be argued that this is a different type of speculative activity from that opposed by some unlisted firms.

[16] Listings of commercial bank securities on the San Francisco Exchange include Anglo-California, Crocker First National, and Wells Fargo.

VARIABLE COMMISSIONS

Unique characteristics of the over-the-counter division of the securities market, other than restricted publicity, can be treated under the heading of distribution procedures proper. Variable commissions (or spreads), dealers acting as principals, and salesmen associated directly with primary markets, all condition the degree of investor interest. They also operate in a manner which tends to equate through time the flow of orders to buy with the flow of orders to sell.

In order to gain insight into the relative advantages of these marketing techniques, let us examine their implications in terms of demand and supply relationships. The assumption is made, based upon empirical observation, that commissions on over-the-counter transactions in common shares are generally higher than those on orders executed in listed issues.[17] Securities salesmen are thus encouraged to make special efforts in the marketing of over-the-counter securities.

If effective, selling effort influences investor preference patterns. Whether the resultant market for over-the-counter stocks is indeed better than that for listed stocks, however, is not ascertainable a priori.[18] To point up the considerations involved, let us examine the case of 2 stocks, designated respectively as A and B. It is presumed that, except for the fact that A is listed and B is not and for the effects thereof, the 2 stocks are identical at the outset.

Since B is traded over-the-counter, its price per share initially exceeds that of A by an amount equal to the difference in the commissions or spreads, say, 3 per cent of selling price.[19] If price and quantity demanded are inversely related—as is normally the case for assets of all types—higher commissions tend to reduce activity through their effect upon security prices. The analysis does not, however, terminate at this point, for the possibility of shifts in demand remains to be considered.

---

[17] See, for example, I. Friend, M. Hamburg, and S. Schor, *Pricing and Price Differentials on Over-the-Counter Markets* (Philadelphia: University of Pennsylvania Press, 1955). According to this report, average customer cost of transferring unlisted common stock from one public customer to another was about 5.7 per cent in 1949 and 5.6 per cent in 1952, as compared with 2.1 per cent for common stock listed on the New York Stock Exchange.

[18] A "better market" is defined simply as one characterized by a larger *average* volume of transactions per unit of time.

[19] Since over-the-counter dealers may act either as principals or agents, the term "commission" is understood to refer henceforth to dealer income accruing from the difference between "bid" and "asked" prices, that is, spreads, as well as that derived from services as agent, that is, commission.

Selling effort can be expected to vary directly with the level of remuneration within wide limits. As a result, B, through the diverse advertising media employed by over-the-counter traders, will be brought to the attention of investors who might otherwise not have considered it. More important, account executives are induced to recommend B in preference to A for inclusion in individual portfolios. To the extent that advice of this nature is accepted, the demand for B increases.

The success of higher commissions in stimulating sales is evidenced by the growth of open-end investment companies in the postwar period.[20] Despite loading charges ranging from 6 to 8 per cent of purchase price, activity in open-end shares substantially exceeds that in closed-end shares. Closed-end shares, whose prices are consistently less than asset value per share and whose transfer costs are far below the loading charges on open-end shares, have nonetheless represented relative bargains during this period.

Systematic presentation of the preceding considerations is permitted by the introduction of two elasticity concepts. Let us define price elasticity of demand (E_p) as the relationship between a percentage change in quantity demanded and the corresponding percentage change in price and promotional elasticity of demand (E_i) as the relationship between a relative change in quantity demanded and the corresponding relative change in commission per share. The relative difference in the market for B and A can then be viewed as:

$$(1) \qquad \frac{\triangle q}{q} = E_p \; \frac{\triangle p}{p} + E_i \; \frac{\triangle i}{i} \; ,$$

where

$$\frac{\triangle q}{q} \quad , \quad \frac{\triangle p}{p} \; , \text{and} \frac{\triangle i}{i}$$

respectively are the proportionate changes in quantity demanded, price per share, and commission per share and where $\triangle p - \triangle i$ equals zero.

The degree of promotional elasticity depends upon both the effectiveness of additional selling effort and the increment in selling effort per unit of increases in commission. Normally, E_i can be noticeably smaller than E_p and still occasion a better market for B than A. To illustrate this point, assume that E_p is one and that

---

[20] For further evidence of the importance of incentives, see "Indifferent Salesmen Impede New Instalment Stock-Buying Program," *Wall Street Journal* (Pacific Coast edition), February 3, 1954.

$\triangle$p/p and $\triangle$i/i for B over A are respectively 3 per cent and 100 per cent. Under these circumstances, the market for B will exceed that for A, provided E_i exceeds .03.

The implicit presumption has thus far been that commissions charged in over-the-counter trading are similar in all relevant respects except amount to those involved in the transfer of listed stocks. In reality, commissions imposed on over-the-counter stocks exhibit much less uniformity than those levied against listed issues.[21] The basis for this difference lies in the fact that the over-the-counter segment is a negotiated market with dealers frequently acting as principals. Wherever dealers serve as principals, commissions in over-the-counter trading are simply the spreads between "bid" and "asked" prices and may vary from transaction to transaction.

The combined presence of restricted publicity and variable commissions suggests the likelihood of price discrimination in over-the-counter trading. That is to say, some attempt may be made by security dealers to charge what the traffic will bear. If such is the case, average prices and average commissions cease to be completely relevant in determining the importance of the first term ($E_p[\triangle$p/p]) of equation (1) as it applies to B. Rather, prices and increments to commissions at the margin assume significance. The presence of price discrimination, if it exists, implies that commissions at the margin may be little higher (and conceivably lower) for over-the-counter shares than for listed stocks. This factor strengthens the possibility that the market for B will surpass that for A.

Although the market for B need not be larger than that for A, the analysis up to this point indicates that such a result is likely to obtain. Listed stocks feature, however, at least two additional compensating advantages which merit attention. In the first place, information about transactions in listed shares is disseminated quickly and widely throughout the trading area by means of ticker service and comprehensive newspaper coverage. Consistently active listings thus receive continuous publicity, whereas others receive publicity in accordance with their frequency of transactions.

The essential point is that the potential influence of augmented promotional effort by security dealers is conditioned by the nature of the security in question. As a result of the public reporting (when listed) of price and volume data and of product advertising, the

---

[21] If a part of the specialists' spread is included in the cost of transferring listed issues, the total transfer cost for listed stocks exhibits some variability, but presumably less than that for over-the-counter issues.

widely distributed shares of well-established corporations require little selling effort. As the distribution of holdings narrows and the reputation of the firm becomes less well-known, the probable benefit of increased selling effort rises.

In the second place, the number of security salesmen interested in A may often exceed those concerned with B. The reason is that organized exchanges represent collections of brokerage firms which channel orders of the floor of the exchange. To obtain the interest of salesmen other than their own, over-the-counter dealers maintaining primary markets for B must either allow the spread between the inside and outside prices to exceed the minimum commission rate or promise reciprocating business.[22] Wherever the number of salesmen interested in A is greater than those concerned with B, the advantage of higher selling effort per salesman may be partly offset.

Whether the market for B is better or worse than that for A, the income accruing to security dealers from B is likely to surpass that from A. Commissions constitute a relatively small proportion of a security's selling price. Unless the demand for the stock in question is highly elastic, a given percentage increase in commissions will not elicit an equivalent relative decline in quantity demanded (even in the absence of added selling effort). The consequence is that the over-the-counter dealers most closely associated with the issuers of B will ordinarily advise against listing, whatever the market impact of such action.

DEALERS AS PRINCIPALS

The fact that over-the-counter dealers often act as principals (rather than agents) and take positions in over-the-counter shares introduces yet another effect upon demand and supply relationships. By assuming long and short positions security traders endeavor to stabilize security prices through time. Whenever the quantity demanded at the going price is substantially different from the quantity supplied, security dealers can eliminate the discrepancy by offering to buy or sell on their own account, provided the risk is not excessive.

Activity of this type is analogous to the function assumed by specialists on the organized exchanges. It may also—under certain

---

[22] The former is difficult since customers can always request their brokers to act as agents, that is, to charge the inside price plus the commission rate.

conditions—resemble speculation. Since our present purpose is to ascertain the competitive advantages of the over-the-counter segment as contrasted with organized exchanges, the question naturally arises as to which division of the securities market can accomplish the market stabilization task most efficaciously.

The answer is believed to depend upon relative incentives and abilities to take positions. For incentives, the decision is probably in favor of over-the-counter dealers. Dealers can, without fear of reprisal from the NASD, adjust markups in accordance with the degree of risk. Because of the relatively high commissions in over-the-counter trading and of investment banking responsibilities, security dealers may, in addition, be induced by longer run considerations to maintain suitable markets. In brief, over-the-counter firms are less subject to regulation (i.e., have greater flexibility) and have more future profits involved than specialists on organized exchanges.[23]

With respect to abilities to take positions, the decision also rests in favor of over-the-counter dealers. In the first place, a multiplicity of brokerage firms may exhibit interest in unlisted stocks, as contrasted with the single specialist assigned to any given listing on regional exchanges. Between April 1, 1954, and July 1, 1954, for example, some 64 and 62 brokerage firms respectively furnished the National Quotation Bureau with "bid" and "offered" quotations for Arizona Public Service and Foremost Dairies. Although these cases are exceptional and include quotations from different regional agencies of the same national brokerage firm in some instances, they are indicative of the numbers which may be involved.

Since data on the size of specialist firms are lacking, we can only speculate as to their relative availability of capital. It is nonetheless apparent that the larger brokerage firms are financially able to take longer positions than are the specialists. It is also evident that brokerage firms have greater resources at their disposal on the basis of sheer numbers alone.

A second factor affecting the relative ability of over-the-counter firms to assume positions is the direct contact with security salesmen. The effect of their presence is to reduce the risk of position-taking. As positions rise, selling effort, as well as spreads, can be adjusted accordingly in order to prevent undue accumulations.

[23] The fact that specialists are in a sense passive, rather than active, agents will be considered subsequently.

Because of their separation from the retailing function, specialists can modify positions only by changing their "bid" and "asked"
prices.[24] The result is that fluctuations in the prices of listed stocks
may at times exceed those in the prices of equivalent over-the-
counter issues and the cost of buying and selling listed shares, as
reflected in the specialist's spread and the broker's commission,
may in some instances be greater than that in connection with similar unlisted securities.

In positioning, as well as in selling effort, the competitive advantages of over-the-counter trading need not be as substantial as they
appear at first glance. Whenever several dealers are interested in a
single unlisted stock, both positioning and selling effort may be
uncoördinated among firms and thus less effective than would
otherwise be the case. Wherever one dealer maintains primary
markets in numerous securities, the argument that some issues must
inevitably be neglected gains force.

Market partitioning may present less of a problem to specialists
on regional exchanges than to over-the-counter dealers. Few of the
San Francisco listings which were surveyed report significant off-
the-floor trading. To the extent that the volume of orders handled
by specialists exceeds those by individual dealers, positions required
to service the market adequately are likely to be relatively lower
for specialists than for over-the-counter traders. As in the case of
selling effort, however, the importance of this point varies directly
with the size of the issuing firm and the distribution of its stock.

A further consideration, suggested by the president of the San
Francisco Exchange, might be raised, although its significance cannot be determined. It is that specialists are obligated to maintain
markets at *some* price whatever the condition of the securities market. In contrast, over-the-counter dealers may, if the risk becomes
excessive, simply cease to trade in stocks for which they previously
created primary markets.[25]

Although such factors as selling effort and positioning have been
examined, the basic advantage of over-the-counter distribution
procedures is flexibility. Procedures can be adjusted to the specific
requirements of individual issues and of single transactions. The
principal question in ascertaining the willingness of dealers to make
special effort is the level of anticipated profits. Although the pro-

---

[24] Minor alternatives, such as personal contact with brokerage firms, are of course
available.

[25] It should, however, be observed that over-the-counter dealers are not without
certain responsibilities.

cedures of regional exchanges are not entirely rigid, changes are relatively difficult to initiate in that they must be approved by the membership.

COMPENSATING ACTION BY REGIONAL EXCHANGES

Let us, for reasons specified above, accept the proposition that the flexible, and in part unique, marketing characteristics of over-the-counter trading favor decisions by regional corporations *not* to list their securities. The term "regional" is understood to apply to publicly owned companies whose issues either do not qualify for listing on the New York Stock Exchange or would be featured by inadequate activity on the national exchanges. The problem then becomes one of determining what compensating steps, if any, might be taken by regional exchanges.

COMMISSION SCHEDULES

The matter of satisfactory broker interest in regional listings is difficult to resolve. If it is assumed that the incentives should correspond to the selling effort required, two sets of minimum commission schedules might well be established by regional exchanges; a low rate schedule for the stocks of nationally known corporations which in effect sell themselves, and a high rate schedule for the securities of medium-size, regional companies. The objective underlying a dual rate structure is not only to awaken the interest of member firms in existing listings, but also to reduce opposition of some brokerage firms at least to the listing of qualified issues presently traded over-the-counter. Criteria for applying the two schedules would presumably take into account the number of shareholders and the size of the firm.

In setting the commission schedules, the low rate schedule need not (and, indeed, cannot) be far different from that presently employed by the New York Stock Exchange. Some experimentation may be necessary to ascertain the appropriate high rate schedule. It can, however, be based upon normal spreads in over-the-counter trading *less* the cost of services provided by the regional exchanges.

At least three objections may be raised against the proposal for dual rate schedules. One is that it does not wholly offset the competitive advantage of over-the-counter trading. Within the boundaries imposed by uniformity of procedures, dual rates nonetheless eliminate part of the differential.

A second difficulty, expressed by the president of the San Francisco Exchange, is that dual rates may encourage off-the-floor trading in regional issues. The point is made that over-the-counter dealers can, if higher rates are levied, profitably trade in listed stocks with spreads narrower than the current spreads maintained by specialists, *plus* the increased commissions.

The answer to this consideration is believed to lie in the factors influencing the margin between the "bid" and "asked" prices quoted by specialists. Since the principal determinants are the risk involved and the interval for which funds are likely to be unavailable for other uses, spreads can be expected to move directly with transactions volume. If augmented dealer interest results from higher commission schedules and activity thereby increases, it follows that the risk in assuming positions will be reduced and the turnover of funds raised. The anticipated result is lower margins between "bid" and "asked" quotations by specialists.

Whether the amount by which spreads on regional listings are narrowed as a consequence of increased volume will equal the increment to commissions is yet another matter. The prospect of competition from over-the-counter dealers may impel specialists to offset approximately the change in commission rates. Even if it does not, however, transactions on the floor of the exchange may still increase because of the large number of exchange members, relative to over-the-counter dealers, which are likely to become interested. In the event that the necessary margins maintained by specialists, together with commissions, exceed over-the-counter spreads at corresponding levels of activity, there is serious doubt as to the propriety of listing the security in question.

A third problem relates to the difficulty of justifying dual rate schedules to the investing public. In this case, the problem appears to be one of disseminating information. It may be argued that, if the economies of scale are truly significant for regional exchanges, either the total cost of buying and selling securities (as measured above) will decline, or more than proportional increases in services will accrue. It also may be pointed out that the existing commission schedules are not truly uniform among securities and that a dual rate system merely discloses something which lies concealed at present.

With respect to the latter point, the commission rate is based upon the market value of a round-lot rather than upon the total size of the transaction. Assuming the transaction involves multiples of 100 shares, the rate is determined by multiplying the 100-shares commission by the number of round-lots bought or sold. This procedure applies to stocks selling at 50 or more cents per share. The consequence, as indicated earlier, is that transactions in low-priced issues which are likely to involve multiples of 100 shares are discriminated against.

Commission schedules currently adopted by organized exchanges can thus be viewed as multiple rate systems in which the market prices of listed stocks play decisive roles. To the extent that regional issues are predominantly low-priced, existing commission rates encourage greater broker interest in regional stocks. The obvious criticisms are, however, that not all regional securities are low-priced and that dollar stocks often require less selling effort than $10 (and higher) shares.

The preceding remarks not only provide a sound basis for justifying dual rate schedules to the investing public; they also suggest a desirable amendment to minimum commission schedules. It is that rates should be determined by the total value of the transaction rather than by the value of a round-lot. The proposed revision would recognize the relatively fixed nature of brokerage expenses, eliminate the arbitrary multiplicity of rates, and permit more effective competition with the over-the-counter segment.

Because of its relative insignificance, the point that over-the-counter dealers do not distinguish between round- and odd-lots has not been emphasized. If the proposition is accepted that minor changes can assume importance when added together, it nonetheless might well be argued that this distinction should be abolished for regional issues.[20] No problems of great consequence are expected to arise from this procedural adjustment. The odd-lot function is already associated with the specialist function on regional exchanges. In addition, regional ticker systems are at present far from being overburdened.

MARKET MAINTENANCE

The matter of market maintenance, that is, of willingness and ability on the part of specialists to assume positions, has already been partly resolved by regional exchanges. The dual responsibility

[20] See, for example, A. Pinney, "The Plight of the Stock Exchange," *Analysts Journal,* Vol. 10, No. 4 (August, 1954), p. 101.

given specialists for both round- and odd-lot trading in their assigned stocks has been noted. The effect of combining functions
is to reduce the risk of assuming positions and to elevate the status
of regional specialists relative to their over-the-counter counterparts. Resources available for positioning are enhanced by the fact
that the several specialists may be members of the same firm. As a
result, funds in excess of the capital requirements for individual
specialists may be available for shifting from stock to stock, provided the needs for positioning do not arise all at once.

The ability of over-the-counter dealers to equate the flow of
orders to buy and sell by means of direct selling effort and thus
to limit the size of their positions has also been counteracted to
some extent by regional exchanges. Installation of broadcast facilities on the exchange floor enables regional specialists to commu-
nicate directly with subscribing firms. Whenever orders to buy
(sell) are not matched by orders to sell (buy), the information can
be disseminated to member firms in the hope of eliciting offsetting
orders.

VOLUME AUGMENTATION

Several possibilities exist for augmenting the flow of buy and sell
orders. One, already undertaken by the San Francisco Exchange,
is to enlarge the membership. A second suggestion is for member
firms to pay the same percentage of their fees to reputable outside
brokers for originating and servicing business as are paid to their
own production employees.[27]

This amendment, currently adopted only by the Los Angeles
and San Francisco exchanges, could well rank among the most
important. Nonmember firms outnumber member firms by ten
to one and have a very direct interest at present in diverting both
orders and listings away from the organized exchanges. By sharing
fees when the occasion arises, the conflict between over-the-counter
trading and trading on organized exchanges might be diminished
perceptibly.

Since regional exchanges constitute one form of marketing co-
operatives, direct advertising of the product, that is, regional listings, is offered as a further possibility. As a matter of fact, joint
promotion is likely to be more efficient—so far as it goes—than
individual effort on the part of over-the-counter dealers. The ab-

---

[27] Pinney, *op. cit.*

sence of experience in the joint advertising of shares precludes specific comments about its potentiality. Suffice it to say, however, that similar programs have proven successful in other fields.

Regulatory restrictions may limit experimentation in this area. It is nonetheless reasonable to expect that regional exchanges would be permitted to distribute much more information about regional listings than is currently given. Since the value of institutional advertising depends upon the quality of the product, opportunities for coöperative promotion will vary in accordance with the abilities of regional exchanges to obtain satisfactory listings.

OTHER POSSIBILITIES

Other steps which might be taken by regional exchanges are conditioned largely upon the concern of member firms over the future of regional exchanges. As has been done by the New York Stock Exchange, capital requirements for specialists can be raised. A pertinent question in this connection is of course whether the remuneration is worth the added investment. As exemplified by the American Stock Exchange in connection with Pantepec Oil, exchanges can also maintain prices in individual stocks in exceptional circumstances by underwriting specialist activity.[28] If necessary, funds can be earmarked for this purpose.

Important as these considerations are, questions of continuous contact with corporations and prestige appear to be even more crucial. In repeated contact with corporations, brokerage firms have distinct advantages over regional exchanges. Through their investment banking and over-the-counter operations, such firms have initial, personal, and continued relations with companies. Without drastic changes in the structure of the securities market, little can be done by regional exchanges to remove this advantage.

In prestige, perhaps something can be done. Prestige is influenced by size and aggressive action. Size in turn is related to ability to obtain new listings and willingness to merge with other regional exchanges. Since the ability to acquire new listings is presently at low ebb, an initial step may well involve the merger and consolidation of regional exchanges.

Aggressive action refers essentially to the fact that regional ex-

---

[28] "Winchell's Stock Tips Investigated," *San Francisco Chronicle*, March 5, 1955. In the case of Pantepec Oil Stock it is reported that "market officials pegged the opening price at $8 ⅞ by getting the specialist handling the stock to offer 144,000 shares at that price."

changes should endeavor to assume active roles in the securities market. If they have something to offer—and presumably they do—it should be publicized.

THE MATTER OF CONFLICTING INTERESTS

Only passing reference has been thus far made to the fact that member firms of regional exchanges are ordinarily confronted with conflicting interests. Most member firms derive income from both the execution of orders in listed issues and over-the-counter trading. Evidence of their dual activities is found in the overwhelming percentage of member firms which belong to the National Association of Security Dealers. Of the 282 members of the Midwest Exchange, 275 belong to the NASD; of the 123 members of the Philadelphia–Baltimore Exchange, 117 are associated with the NASD; of the 53 members of the San Francisco Exchange, 46 are linked to the NASD; and of the 50 members of the Los Angeles Exchange, 48 are NASD members.[29]

The relative profitability of over-the-counter, as opposed to listed, trading varies of course among brokerage firms. To the extent that income from over-the-counter transactions assumes importance, however, member firms may be reluctant to initiate steps which might affect the lucrativeness of over-the-counter trading. As a consequence, problems are likely to arise in obtaining approval for significant changes in the procedures of regional exchanges.

Information is unavailable as to the normal division of income between listed and over-the-counter trading for brokerage firms. The case of one medium-size firm which is a member of both the New York Exchange and the California exchanges can nonetheless be cited to demonstrate the potential importance of over-the-counter transactions. During the first half of 1955, registered representatives of this firm derived nearly two-fifths of their gross income from preëxisting over-the-counter issues, more than one-third from underwriting activity, and less than one-seventh from listed stocks.[30]

The significance of this point is difficult to evaluate. It is reasonable to suppose that member firms hesitate to endorse the regional listing of over-the-counter issues in which they have personal stakes. An important effect of listing is to eliminate the monopoly privileges associated with the maintenance of primary markets for unlisted stocks.

---

[29] *Stock Market Study Hearings*, 84th Cong., 1st sess. (Washington, 1955), p. 357.
[30] The only other substantial source was the sale of investment company shares.

It is equally legitimate to presume that member firms are inclined to favor the betterment of regional exchanges as long as the matter of vested interests does not arise. The awakened concern of senior partners of member firms in exchange operations, as revealed in discussions with exchange members, and the resultant changes of recent vintage in regional exchange procedures suggest that further innovations may be in store. Definite conclusions cannot be drawn, however, since none of the improvements proposed up to the present time appear to represent major departure from traditional methods.

From a dollars-and-cents point of view, the question of conflicting interests becomes one of losses versus gains. To the extent that exchange members participate actively in the over-the-counter segment, losses accrue from the listing of over-the-counter issues because of narrowed spreads (or commissions) and reduced trading in issues for which they previously maintained primary markets. Gains from listing accrue to member firms through the increased variety of offerings, the reduction in promotional effort required, the shifting of risk to specialists, and the economies of coöperative or joint activity. With the possible exception of reduced selling effort, each of these items is considered elsewhere. If a given stock is suitable for listing, listing can be expected to diminish the necessity of promoting activity therein by virtue of the facts that price and volume data are publicized, financial statements must be prepared periodically and are often summarized in financial publications, and that the status of the exchange upon which the issue is listed frequently influences investor decisions.

Exchange officials attach weight to the matter of conflicting interests, but hesitate to combat it. An official of one regional exchange reveals that the lowering of listing requirements is under consideration for this very reason. His point is that flexible listing standards permit listing by companies with reasonable prospects before the vested interests of over-the-counter dealers assume such proportions that listing on regional exchanges is difficult, if not impossible. In other cases, hope is commonly expressed that legislation requiring corporations whose securities are traded over-the-counter to report to the Securities and Exchange Commisison will induce many companies to take the initiative in listing.

VI

Merger Activity

During the past decade, mergers—like penicillium—have been proposed as cures for a variety of ailments. Estimates of mergers and acquisitions during this period run as high as 10,000.[1] A Federal Trade Commission table, which is admittedly incomplete and has been withdrawn from circulation, records 4,371 consolidations between 1945 and the middle of 1954.

In the light of this activity, it seems natural to ask whether the status of regional exchanges might not also be elevated by means of merger. That the members and officials of some regional exchanges believe the answer to be in the affirmative is evidenced by the fact that at least two exchange consolidations have taken place in recent years. The Midwest Stock Exchange, representing a combination of the Chicago, Cleveland, Minneapolis–St. Paul, and St. Louis exchanges, commenced operations in December, 1949. The Philadelphia Stock Exchange united with the Baltimore Exchange in March, 1949, and with the Washington Exchange in October, 1953. At the time of this writing (August, 1956), moreover, the San Francisco and Los Angeles exchanges are preparing to join forces.

Potential benefits accruing from the consolidation of regional exchanges appear to fall into two groups. One relates to reductions in the ratios of exchange expenses to volume traded. If fixed costs are a substantial element of total outlays, lower costs on a per unit basis may be achieved. The other concerns increments to the aggregate volume of transactions. If additional corporations can be induced to list their securities and if members can be encouraged to take greater interest in exchange activities, the results may be noteworthy.

A review of recent merger activity appears desirable as an initial step to focus attention both upon the probable importance of these

---

[1] "Why Merge," *Wall Street Journal* (Pacific Coast edition), March 10, 1955.

advantages and upon the mechanics of unifying regional exchanges. Consideration is given thereafter to the arguments for and against combining the California exchanges.

Of prime interest is the current plan to unite the San Francisco and Los Angeles exchanges. From this viewpoint alone, the experience of other regional exchanges is invaluable. Of lesser—but nonetheless substantial—concern is the number of regional exchanges whose existence is, or might become, justifiable. The proposition which we seek to confirm or deny is that, for the present at least, the East, Midwest, and Far West can each support effectively no more than one *major* regional exchange. Whether the East, in view of the location of the national exchanges, really merits its own regional exchange is not immediately apparent.

MERGER OF THE MIDWESTERN EXCHANGES

Although conceived as a plan to consolidate all Midwestern exchanges, the Midwest Exchange proposal was approved by neither the Detroit nor the Cincinnati Exchange.[2] Uncertainty of outcome and matters of local pride apparently accounted for the adverse decisions. The door nonetheless remains open for these 2 exchanges to unite with the Midwest Exchange and to improve further its status.

The Midwest Exchange is unusual in that branch offices are located in Cleveland and St. Louis. Continuous contact is maintained between the branches and the Chicago trading floor by teletype. Stock quotations and orders to buy and sell move over this network of wires. Each branch office records price changes on a quotation board. In obtaining quotations and placing orders, brokers in Cleveland and St. Louis deal directly with their respective branch offices. In Minneapolis, which has no branch, members are connected directly with the trading floor by teletype.

Membership in the Midwest Exchange now numbers 400 and is not confined to brokerage firms operating in the area bounded by Chicago, Cleveland, Minneapolis, and St. Louis.[3] In addition to the large New York firms, member firms are located in such places as Texas, South Carolina, and New Orleans. Clearing by mail, a procedure originated by the Midwest Exchange, permits distant firms to transact business on the Midwest Exchange without the creation of branch offices in Chicago.[4] It also enables the Cleve-

---

[2] *Wall Street Journal* (Pacific Coast edition), December 2, 1949.
[3] Of the total, approximately 300 represent brokerage firms.
[4] The present out-of-town clearing membership approximates 130 firms.

TABLE 23

CONSOLIDATED STATEMENT OF INCOME AND EXPENSE FOR THE MIDWEST STOCK EXCHANGE
(For the years ending Nov. 30, 1954 and 1953)

Income from operations	Year ended		Increase[a] (decrease)
	Nov. 30, 1954	Nov. 30, 1953	
Members' dues....................	$200,000.00	$190,000.00	$ 10,000.00
Net commission fees................	103,727.55	71,506.89	32,220.66
Security listing fees.................	36,000.00	37,750.00	(1,750.00)
Clearing house income..............	180,351.00	127,976.45	52,374.55
Other income.....................	41,863.37	37,428.95	4,434.42
	$561,941.92	$464,662.29	$ 97,279.63
Operating expenses Midwest Stock Exchange salaries of officers and employees (exclusive of branch offices)...............	$203,054.21	$185,961.73	$ 17,092.48
Rent...........................	43,567.50	40,200.00	3,367.50
Cleveland office expenses..........	25,486.44	21,130.41	4,356.03
St. Louis office expenses...........	24,047.05	23,383.84	663.21
Other operating expenses..........	97,237.50	86,476.77	10,760.73
Midwest Stock Clearing Corp......	174,338.98	126,095.17	48,243.81
	$567,731.68	$483,247.92	$ 84,483.76
Other income	$ (5,789.76)	$(18,585.63)	$ 12,795.87
Interest on Investments..........	27,759.44	28,080.41	(320.97)
Net income..................	$ 21,969.68	$ 9,494.78	$ 12,474.90

SOURCE: Midwest Stock Exchange, *Annual Report*, 1954, p. 6.
[a] No provision for income taxes was necessary in either 1954 or 1953.

land, Minneapolis, and St. Louis factions of the initial consolidation to remain in the same offices utilized before the merger.

OPERATING COSTS

Whether operating costs, calculated on a per-share basis, changed drastically as a result of the merger is problematical. Expenses per unit tend to be reduced by virtue both of increased activity and of the fact that the branch offices require about half of the space formerly occupied by the local exchanges.[5] Branch office out-

---

[5] It should be pointed out in connection with increased volume that a sizable proportion of the change which has occurred in the past five years might well have taken place even without the merger.

lays amounted only to 10 per cent of total operating costs for the fiscal years ending November 30, 1952 and 1953.

Per-share expenses tend to be raised by expanded services and by the need for continuous communication between the trading floor and its appendages. Additional services of a direct character include such things as the installation of broadcasting facilities and the carrying out of bookkeeping operations for odd-lot firms located away from Chicago. Indirect services have been provided through augmented public relations activities and closer contact with regional companies.

Operating expenses for the fiscal years ending November 30, 1953 and 1954, are shown in table 23. The interesting feature of these data is their relatively insignificant proportions. In each of the two years, operating costs amounted to slightly more than three cents per share traded. Expressed as a percentage of dollar volume, expenses approximated one-tenth of 1 per cent for this period. Although the importance of operating outlays increases substantially when related to commissions earned by members, it may nonetheless be concluded that the effect of consolidation upon transactions volume is far more crucial than its influence upon costs.

To illustrate this point, let us assume that operating expenses amount to 10 per cent of the commissions earned by member firms and that commissions in turn average 1 per cent of dollar volume. Under these circumstances a 50 per cent reduction in costs increases membership profits by only 5 per cent. Whereas, a 10 per cent rise in dollar transactions would augment profits by 9 per cent, provided that added activity is attributable solely to the efforts of the exchange. As can be observed from table 23, the assumed figures are not far different from those of the Midwest Exchange.

EFFECT UPON VOLUME

In the matter of enlarged volume through the combination of midwestern exchanges, officials of the predecessor exchanges envisaged growth through merger to assume two forms. They anticipated that the improved status of the Midwest Exchange, together with aggressive action and transfer of inactive memberships, would induce additional companies to list their issues. They also expected that increased opportunities for profit would encourage members to take greater interest in the affairs of the new exchange.

Insufficient time has elapsed since its inception for us to judge conclusively the effectiveness of the Midwest Stock Exchange in fostering additional volume. In his recent statement before the Senate Committee on Banking and Currency, however, James E. Day, president of the Midwest Exchange, expresses the opinion that the success of the new exchange has been substantial.[6] As supporting evidence, he points out that, during the last five years, the Midwest Exchange, on an annual basis, has exhibited a greater increment to both share and dollar volume than any other domestic exchange. Mr. Day also stresses the significant increase in the trading of regional issues. The year before the consolidation, transactions in local issues totaled 1,961,000 shares, whereas in 1954, they amounted to 4,557,000 shares, a growth of 143 per cent.

Data contained in the *Annual Report* of the Midwest Exchange for 1954 reveal that the average annual increase in shares traded on the Midwest Exchange has been 107 per cent during the past five years, as contrasted with 63 per cent for all exchanges. In terms of dollar value, the increase amounted to 151 per cent for Midwest, as compared with 96 per cent for all exchanges. In relation to the Midwest Exchange's total activity, the volume handled by branch offices has risen in every year since the merger. In 1954, the Cleveland office transacted three times the 1949 volume of the former Cleveland Exchange. The St. Louis office in turn originated more than four times the share volume of the old St. Louis Exchange in the year preceding the merger.

The percentage breakdown of the dollar amount of business transacted on United States security exchanges is shown in table 24 and appears consistent with the thesis that consolidation has benefited the midwestern exchanges. The ratio of dollar volume on the Midwest Exchange to aggregate activity on all domestic exchanges rose from 2.35 per cent in 1950 to 2.42 per cent in 1954. Although this increment is not impressive in itself, it compares favorably with the behavior of both the American Exchange and other leading regional exchanges. For these security exchanges, the tendency has been for relative positions to decline between 1950 and 1954.

NEW LISTING POTENTIAL

Directly related to the question of added volume is that of ability to keep existing listings and to acquire new ones. In this connection, Mr. Day comments that the former Chicago Exchange was

---

[6] *Factors Affecting the Buyer and Selling of Equity Securities, Hearings,* The Committee on Banking and Currency, 84th Cong., 1st sess. (Washington, 1955), p. 222.

losing 10 to 12 issues annually before 1948.[7] Subsequent to the formation of the Midwest Exchange, average yearly losses have been reduced to 3 or 4.

The achievements of the Midwest Exchange in obtaining new listings of regional issues have been, as mentioned previously, somewhat less noteworthy thus far. Recent acquisitions include Henry C. Lytton and Northern Illinois Gas, originally an affiliate of Commonwealth Edison. Some indication of improved status can be found in the statement of the president of Peabody Coal to the effect that the "market for Peabody stock exists almost entirely in the Chicago area—if we had it to do over again, we would doubtless list here rather than in New York."[8]

Despite favorable evidence of this kind, it is apparent that the task of encouraging further regional companies to list their issues continues to be arduous. The conclusion is that the combination of midwestern exchanges has produced positive results. Whether the Midwest Exchange reflects the full potential of regional exchanges as yet, however, is doubtful. The Midwest Exchange continues to rely heavily upon multiply traded issues. In 1954, for example, transactions in multiple listings amounted to 14,543,000 shares, as compared with only 4,557,000 shares for local issues.[9] Local and dual system issues currently number 120 and 200 respectively. As long as these relationships obtain, the chief objective of the Midwest Exchange cannot truly be regarded as one of maintaining primary markets for regional issues.

The continued and perhaps increasing dependence of the Midwest Exchange upon multiply traded issues is reflected in its emphasis upon the fact that Illinois has no stock-transfer tax. Since the inception of the Midwest Exchange, some 55 tax-free transfer agencies have been established at the insistence of the exchange for issues traded thereon. These transfer agencies handled transactions for all but 19 of the 200 or more multiply traded issues.

CONSOLIDATION OF THE EASTERN EXCHANGES

Earlier in the same year that the merger of Midwestern exchanges occurred, the Philadelphia and Baltimore stock exchanges united to form the Philadelphia–Baltimore Exchange. This consolidation, together with an aggressive program initiated to stimulate trading,

---

[7] J. R. Elliott, Jr., "Regional Exchanges," *Barron's* (June 27, 1955), p. 28.
[8] *Ibid.*
[9] *Hearings, op. cit.*

was viewed as an experimental step away from the status of a strictly local exchange and in the direction of regional independence.[10]

UNIFICATION PROCEDURE

The method by which the combination was effected involved the liquidation of the Baltimore Exchange and the distribution of its assets among the 35 outstanding memberships. Seventeen Baltimore firms then proceeded to purchase "seats" on the new exchange. These memberships were made available by the Philadelphia Exchange through the acquisition of four in the open market and the issuance of the 13 treasury memberships remaining out of the 200 authorized.

Factors contributing to the smoothness of the Baltimore operation included the establishment of direct telephonic communication from Baltimore to the trading floor and the provision for out-of-town clearances by the Stock Clearing Corporation.[11] A lamp and key switchboard receives the orders of Baltimore firms and transmits them directly to Philadelphia. Transactions are cleared through the Baltimore office.

That the officials and members of the Philadelphia–Baltimore Exchange believed the initial merger to be successful is evidenced by subsequent action on the part of the Exchange. On October 1, 1951, a Washington office was opened with facilities similar to those provided by the Baltimore office. Member firms in Washington were thus afforded the opportunity of executing orders in more than 200 stocks not listed on the Washington Exchange, and pressure was exerted on the Washington Exchange to join forces with the Philadelphia–Baltimore Exchange.

On October 15, 1953, the Washington Exchange became a part of the Philadelphia–Baltimore Exchange. Absorption of the Baltimore and Washington exchanges has brought 31 new listings to Philadelphia. The issues of 13 corporations were listed by virtue of the Baltimore merger. Eighteen other listings, together with trading in 12 bank stocks, resulted from the establishment of the Washington branch.

Of greater significance to the Philadelphia–Baltimore Exchange, in connection with the Washington merger, is the fact that combination strengthened appreciably its potential for expansion south-

[10] R. Trigger, "Another Philadelphia First—The Oldest Stock Exchange in America," *Investment and Dealer's Digest* (Special Issue, March 10, 1952), Sect. II, pp. 19–21.
[11] *Ibid.*, p. 21.

ward.[12] In the words of Frank L. Newburger, Jr., president of the Philadelphia–Baltimore Exchange:[13]

We have grown from a local exchange, serving one large city, to a truly regional exchange serving four of the country's 12 largest cities. In addition by serving the Nation's capital, which is the gateway to South Atlantic Seaboard, we have opened up a territory from which we plan to interest new members in addition to those who have already joined our exchange.

The fourth city to which reference is made in the preceding quotation is Pittsburgh. Effective January 1, 1955, arrangements were made to link the trading floors of the Philadelphia–Baltimore and Pittsburgh exchanges by direct telephone wire and to permit the 64 members of the Pittsburgh Exchange to become associate members of the Philadelphia–Baltimore Exchange.[14] By the end of January, 30 members of the Pittsburgh Exchange had availed themselves of this opportunity. The ultimate objective of this step is consolidation of the two exchanges.

Expansion northward is apparently not contemplated by officials and members of the Philadelphia–Baltimore Exchange. Alexander Biddle, executive vice-president of the Philadelphia–Baltimore Exchange, expresses the opinion in correspondence that the Boston Exchange is, and will continue to be, an independent regional exchange, servicing the New England area.

EVALUATION

Evaluation of the merger activity undertaken by the Philadelphia–Baltimore Exchange is difficult. The reason is simply that Eastern regional exchanges are situated in the shadow of the New York exchanges. Regional companies are therefore inclined to go directly from the over-the-counter markets to the New York or American stock exchanges.

Combination has, according to Mr. Biddle, occasioned some reduction in operating costs per share traded, but this consideration does not appear to be of major importance. Consolidation has not, if sales of the Washington branch for 1954 are any indication, greatly increased transactions volume in issues formerly traded on the local exchanges outside of Philadelphia. Activity

---

[12] *Philadelphia–Baltimore Stock Exchange Data*, Philadelphia–Baltimore Stock Exchange, January 31, 1955, Part IV.

[13] "Local Exchange Serves Four Cities," *Philadelphia Enquirer*, January 6, 1955.

[14] "Philadelphia–Baltimore, Pittsburgh Exchanges Plan Close Co-operation," *Wall Street Journal* (East Coast edition), Jan. 6, 1955.

was less for 8 Washington stocks in 1954 than in 1953 and was approximately the same for 13 securities.[15] In only 10 instances did volume rise substantially; and in each case, a high percentage of the orders was executed through the Washington office.

Despite expansion through merger, the proportion of multiply traded issues remains extremely high on the Philadelphia–Baltimore Exchange. Of the 423 stocks traded during 1954, a mere 32 represent local listings. Only 3 of these 32 regional issues are, moreover, actively traded. The term "actively traded" refers in this context to securities which feature an annual volume of trading in excess of 10,000 shares.

The 2 substantial regional listings on the Philadelphia–Baltimore Exchange are Baltimore Transit and Philadelphia Transportation. Philadelphia Transportation, for example, traded 185,646 shares during 1954 and exhibited an annual turnover of almost 26 per cent. If nothing else, these 2 issues demonstrate that—if the quality is right—excellent markets can be maintained on regional exchanges.

As can be seen from table 24, the Philadelphia–Baltimore Exchange has improved its relative position slightly since 1950. Factors contributing to augmented trading in multiple listings apparently include tax savings to customers and high "take-home" commissions, as well as a strong public relations program. The Pennsylvania stock transfer tax is 2 per cent per $100 of par or market value, whichever is less. The New York transfer tax on stocks whose market price is $20 or more is, in comparison, $4 per 100 shares.

Net commissions retained by member firms on round-lot transactions averaged 88.2 per cent for the 20 most active issues in 1954.[16] Net commissions on 50 share lots averaged 90.4 per cent for the same group in 1954. The percentage kept by member firms varies inversely with the selling price of the stock. Floor brokerage fees range from 1.25 cents per share on stocks priced at $1 to $5 to 3.5 cents per share on stocks selling at $100 and more. Clearance charges vary from $.20 per odd-lot item (1 to 9 shares) to $.95 per round-lot item.

The strength of public relations activity is demonstrable in

---

[15] "D. C. Exchange Trade Leaps 47.5% in Year," *Washington Post and Times Herald*, January 8, 1955.

[16] *Philadelphia-Baltimore Stock Exchange Data, op. cit.*, Parts II and III; also "Philadelphia-Baltimore Stock Exchange," *Investment Dealers' Digest* (Special Issue, March 10, 1952), Sect. II, p. 35.

several ways. The Philadelphia–Baltimore Exchange, together with
the Chamber of Commerce, introduced the "Invest in America
Week" idea in 1949. The former Philadelphia Exchange formed
a Public Relations Committee, consisting of prominent people
drawn from finance, industry, and public relations, as early as
1946. Membership on this committee is reported to be a factor
in the decision of the Girard Trust Corn Exchange Bank to use
the facilities of the Stock Clearing Corporation. According to J. M.
Johnston, senior vice-president of the bank:[17]

We started in November, 1948, largely for the purpose of encouraging
the transaction of business on the local exchange. Furthermore, we
have encouraged our brokers to place as many of our orders as possible
on the P-BSE. The experience of several Philadelphia banks has been
such, since that time, that they have been ready to recommend joining
the Stock Clearing Corp. to others.

The point has been made that, unlike the Midwest and West
Coast exchanges, the Philadelphia–Baltimore Exchange services
very few regional issues. As long as this situation continues to
prevail, it cannot be said that the Philadelphia–Baltimore Exchange truly performs the functions of a regional exchange. This
exchange serves rather as an unrecognized and uncoördinated
branch office of the national exchanges.

The conclusion drawn is that, though a few encouraging signs
are present, merger activity has not as yet significantly altered the
status of the Philadelphia–Baltimore Exchange. Some hope exists
for the exchange, provided the anticipated expansion into the south
Atlantic Coast area is successful. Since the South is relatively remote
from the national exchanges, it may ultimately become an excellent source of regional listings. It should be remembered, however,
that the Midwest Exchange too is interested in this region.

UNIFICATION OF THE CALIFORNIA EXCHANGES

The joining together of midwestern exchanges can be viewed as
the first of a logical series of steps designed to reduce the number
of local exchanges to a relatively few important regional exchanges.
A similar point—although one possessing substantially less force—
might be made about the merger activity on the eastern seaboard.
A further step, toward which attention is now directed, concerns

[17] J. M. Johnston, "Public Relations a Key Activity of Philadelphia-Baltimore
Stock Exchange," *Investment Dealers' Digest* (Special Issue, March 10, 1952), Sect. II,
pp. 27–28.

TABLE 24

DOLLAR VOLUME ON U. S. STOCK EXCHANGES FOR SELECTED YEARS, 1935–1955
(in per cent)

Exchange	1935	1940	1950	1954
New York....................	86.64	85.17	85.91	86.23
American.....................	7.83	7.68	6.85	6.79
Midwest.....................	1.32	2.07	2.35	2.42
San Francisco................	.93	1.00	1.18	1.07
Los Angeles.................	.46	.52	1.01	.95
Phila-Balto..................	.68	.92	.92	.94
Boston......................	1.34	1.91	1.12	.89
Detroit.....................	.40	.36	.39	.39
Pittsburgh..................	.20	.19	.11	.14
Cincinnati..................	.04	.09	.11	.10
All others [a]...............	.16	.09	.05	.08
Total all regionals..........	5.53	7.15	7.24	6.98

SOURCE: Securities and Exchange Commission.
[a] All others in 1954 included the Chicago Board of Trade, the San Francisco Mining Exchange, and the stock exchanges in New Orleans, Salt Lake, Spokane, Colorado Springs, Honolulu, Richmond, and Wheeling.

TABLE 25

RELATIONSHIP BETWEEN OPERATING EXPENSES AND ANNUAL VOLUME FOR FIVE
EXCHANGES DURING THE YEARS 1951–1955

Exchange and year	(1) Operating expenses	(2) Share volume	(3) Dollar volume	Ratio of 1 to 2	Ratio of 1 to 3
New York					
1953..........	$9,315,757.19	354,851,325	$14,218,019,435	.026	.0007
1952..........	8,239,811.42	337,805,179	14,720,397,314	.024	.0006
American					
1953..........	$2,134,386.37	102,378,937	1,125,699,042	.021	.0019
1952..........	2,125,637.98	106,237,657	1,273,902,282	.020	.0017
Midwest					
1954..........	567,731.68	18,600,707	644,773,194	.031	.0009
1953..........	483,247.92	15,050,000	479,785,270	.032	.0010
1952..........	446,127.06	13,665,400	446,200,301 [a]	.033	.0010
San Francisco					
1954..........	299,253.54	16,302,149	301,744,115	.018	.0010
1952..........	266,400.00	18,321,000	201,924,405	.014	.0013
1951..........	263,400.00	18,336,000	230,385,676	.014	.0011
Los Angeles					
1954..........	249,442.00 [a]	17,791,645	267,147,396	.014	.0009
1953..........	212,735.00 [a]	10,421,260	163,642,210	.020	.0013

SOURCE: *Annual Reports*, 1952–1955, for the above Exchanges.
[a] Approximations.

the uniting of the San Francisco and Los Angeles exchanges. The basic justification for this combination is, in our opinion, more effective competition with the over-the-counter segment of the securities market.

STEPS TOWARD UNIFICATION

As recently as February, 1955, proposals to combine the two California exchanges appeared to be dormant. In the words of an official of one of these exchanges: "The one great hurdle is area rivalry and pride. Cold logic spurred by less active markets than now exist may ultimately revive and resolve the matter."

On June, 1955, however, the memberships of both exchanges approved the connection of the 2 trading floors by private wire facilities on an experimental basis.[18] The arrangement is similar to that introduced by the Philadelphia–Baltimore and Pittsburgh exchanges at the beginning of 1955. A restricted group of 75 stocks, which are multiply traded on one of the national exchanges and on the Los Angeles and San Francisco exchanges, was initially made available for round-lot purchases or sales on the trading floors of either of the California exchanges after first being offered on the originating exchange. This list of offerings was subsequently expanded to include other multiply traded issues. The stated objective was to keep buy-and-sell orders on the Pacific Coast whenever possible.

Apparently the experiment was deemed successful, for in July, 1956, a plan to form a Pacific Coast Stock Exchange was submitted to members of the San Francisco and Los Angeles exchanges for their approval.[19] The proposed action does not constitute a merger in the strict sense of the word, since each exchange (or division) retains its own property and has its own governing board and president. Government of the new exchange is to be vested in a board of governors comprising the board chairmen and presidents of each division and two other members from each division's board of governors. The chairmanship alternates annually between the chairmen of the two divisions.

Notable changes in the operations of the two exchanges are not expected at the outset. A consolidated list of transactions on the two exchanges is to be issued daily, as opposed to the separate lists

[18] "S.F., L.A. Exchanges Approve Direct Wire Linking Floors," *Wall Street Journal* (Pacific Coast edition), June 14, 1955.

[19] "Two West Coast Exchanges Plan Consolidation," *Wall Street Journal* (Pacific Coast edition), July 31, 1956.

which have been published in the past. The members of each exchange are, in addition, to be afforded what amounts to out-of-town membership privileges on the other exchange.

In essence, then, the new program calls for an extension of the 1955 plan to cover all issues, whether multiply, dually, or locally listed (or traded). According to W. H. Agnew, chairman of the Board of Governors of the San Francisco Exchange: "It will provide distinct possibilities for added income to member firms and greater benefits to the investing public and industries whose securities are listed on either or both exchanges . . ."

In view of what has transpired (and what may well happen in the future), it appears relevant to examine the arguments for unifying the California exchanges. In order to judge the benefit of further steps which might be taken, the assumption of complete— as opposed to partial—integration is introduced. Factors which merit consideration include resultant size (after consolidation) and its effects, similarity of trading area and of issues traded, and benefits derived from coördinated action. These items are discussed in the order listed.

EFFECT OF MERGER UPON SIZE STATUS

As shown in table 24, approximately 1 per cent of the total dollar volume transacted on domestic exchanges is currently handled by each of the California exchanges. For 1953, the dollar magnitude of trading on the San Francisco and Los Angeles exchanges amounted respectively to $204,054,211 and $163,642,210.[20] Physical activity for the same period totaled 17,474,448 shares and 10,481,-260 shares. Merger of the two exchanges would thus give rise to an exchange of dimensions similar to the Midwest Exchange.

According to the 1953 data, physical volume for the California exchanges substantially exceeds that for the Midwest Exchange, although dollar volume favors the Midwest Exchange. Activity in regional listings, expressed in money terms, for the Los Angeles and San Francisco exchanges taken together, may well approach, if not exceed, that for the Midwest Exchange. As reflected in table 2, ratios of multiple trading to total activity are relatively low for the San Francisco and Los Angeles exchanges.

The interesting feature, in this connection, is that unification places the "new" California exchange in an entirely different size

[20] *Summary of Transactions,* San Francisco Stock Exchange, 1953, and *Annual Report,* Los Angeles Stock Exchange, 1954.

category from its predecessors. At present, the San Francisco, Los Angeles, Philadelphia–Baltimore, and Boston exchanges all have approximately the same annual dollar volume. Through consolidation, the West Coast obtains a major regional exchange.

Considerable importance is ascribed to the influence of large increments in size upon exchange status. As pointed out in the preceding chapter, prestige is crucial to successful competition with the over-the-counter segment. Such evidence as is available suggests that the elasticity of prestige in relation to size—although discontinuous—may well exceed one. Wherever substantial increases in activity occur, the position of an exchange is likely to change more than in proportion to variations in its size.

For reasons specified previously, less significance is attached to the effect of augmented activity upon operating costs per share traded than to the impact upon gross commissions. Essentially the same attitude is evinced by a leading official of one California exchange, who states in correspondence: "I question how much operating costs could be reduced but that is a minor factor when related to the income benefits to members."

As might be anticipated, some difference of opinion exists. A top executive of the other California exchange argues that substantial economies may result from consolidation of the two exchanges. This official emphasizes the need for only one trading floor in the event of merger.[21]

Objective evidence of the relation between exchange size and costs of operation can be obtained by means of interexchange comparison. Recent ratios of annual operating expenses to yearly share and dollar volume are shown in table 25 for the 2 national and 3 leading regional exchanges. In terms of operating outlays per share traded, no clear-cut economies of scale appear to exist. With the exception of the Midwest Exchange, per-share costs vary directly with the size of the exchange.

Only when operating costs are expressed as a percentage of dollar volume is the advantage of large-scale operation visible. The fact that the American Stock Exchange fails to conform suggests, however, that the inverse relationship exhibited in this case may simply reflect the ability of the New York Stock Exchange to attract the better quality and higher priced issues. In any event, the union

[21] If the experience of the Midwest and Philadelphia–Baltimore exchanges is any indication, a branch office will be required in addition to the main trading floor. It is therefore unlikely that building costs will be halved.

of West Coast exchanges is unlikely to exert an appreciable influence upon operating outlays per dollar of transactions unless dollar
volume for the "new" exchange far exceeds the combined total
for the existing California exchanges and the integration proceeds
farther than is presently anticipated. This conclusion is based upon
the fact that annual ratios of operating expenses to dollar volume
are not greatly different for the Midwest Exchange from those for
the Los Angeles and San Francisco exchanges.

Certain economies undoubtedly result from expanded operations. It is nonetheless reasonable to suppose that enlarged size
entails additional expenditures. The Philadelphia Exchange, for
example, moved into new quarters upon its merger with the Baltimore Exchange. Advertising and promotional expenditures may
also be increased as activity rises. Although not itemized for either
the American or Midwest exchanges, advertising outlays exceeded
$625,000 for the New York Exchange in both 1952 and 1953.

SIMILARITY OF TRADING AREAS

A second factor which has direct bearing upon merger decisions
is the similarity of trading areas. Whenever 2 exchanges of approximately equal status service the same, or overlapping, markets, certain unfortunate consequences are likely to obtain. Regional
corporations are then confronted not only with the question of
whether to list or not to list, but also with the problem of selecting
the exchange. If the matter is resolved by the dual listing of local
issues, market splitting ensues; and the ability of each exchange
to provide satisfactory markets in such stocks diminishes. In cases
where one exchange is chosen in preference to dual listing, the
balance among regional offerings is adversely affected.[22]

Overlapping of trading areas for the Los Angeles and San Francisco exchanges is evidenced both by their proximity and by the
fact that some 19 issues are dually traded exclusively on these exchanges. An additional 12 stocks are traded on both the California
exchanges and the American Exchange. Annual transactions in
the 19 dual listings are shown in table 26. In a significant number
of instances, the degree of market splitting appears substantial.

Insight into the influence of joint listing upon the ability of
regional specialists to maintain satisfactory markets can also be
obtained from the data contained in table 26. Annual volume for
1953 is less than 25,000 shares for 13 dual listings on the San Fran-

___

[22] Discounts to nonmember firms of course mitigate this problem somewhat.

cisco Exchange and for 6 joint listings on the Los Angeles Exchange. Similar results are exhibited for 1954. If the proposition is correct that adequate markets cannot be provided when transactions in a given security decline below 100 shares per trading day, the case for dual listings is weak wherever this result obtains.

TABLE 26

TRANSACTIONS IN SECURITIES LISTED DUALLY WITH THE LOS ANGELES AND SAN
FRANCISCO STOCK EXCHANGES

(In thousands)

Issue	1953		1954	
	San Francisco	Los Angeles	San Francisco	Los Angeles
Bandini Petroleum	5	149	14	292
Bankline Oil	5	91	15	118
Basin Oil	4	106	3	92
Bishop Oil	26	25	33	49
Bolsa Chica Oil	...	164	41	257
Broadway–Hale Stores	21	102	26	139
Central Eureka	173	3	286	5
Doernbecker Mfg.	18	...	76	...
Electrical Prod.	3	21	1	27
Hancock Oil	39	184	61	400
Intex Oil	59	90	49	124
Norris Oil	13	196	9	143
Holly Development	23	102	28	132
Occidental Petroleum	44	27	22	17
Pac. Clay Products (Old)	1	2	a	18
Pac. Clay Products (New)	...	9	8	18
Pacific Indemnity	...	6	...	8
Reserve Oil and Gas	9	113	4	207
So. Cal. Gas	10	19	10	23
So. California Petroleum	26	72	44	135

SOURCE: San Francisco Exchange, *Summary of Transactions, 1953 and 1954;* Los Angeles Exchange, *Report for the Years 1953 and 1954.*
a Less than 500 shares.

In the study of absorption potential, the appropriate time unit—as observed previously—is the trading day. As a consequence, examination of daily volume, as well as annual activity, is relevant. The degree of market splitting which occurs at any particular time may be significant even though yearly trading in any given dual listing on one regional exchange overwhelms that on the others.

Daily transactions in 19 issues, jointly traded on the San Francisco and Los Angeles exchanges, are shown in table 27 for the two-week period covering April 15, 1955, to April 28, 1955, inclusive.

Daily volume in 13 stocks, listed on both of these exchanges and on the American Exchange, is also recorded therein for the same interval. Although the period examined is too brief to permit the drawing of definite conclusions, the influence of segmentation appears noteworthy for at least one-third of the dually traded issues. Fragmentation also possesses significance for approximately half of the triply traded stocks shown in table 27.

Based upon these data, consolidation of the 2 California exchanges offers three potential benefits. The ability of specialists to create good markets in these issues can be expected to improve—in some cases substantially. Elimination of the weaker markets should provide better service to investors and result in greater interest on their part. For triply traded issues, the "new" California exchange might become the primary market to the extent that trading is concentrated on the West Coast. For 4 of 13 issues, shown in table 27, combined activity on the California exchanges exceeds that on the American Exchange for the two-week period.

Despite the existence of dual listings and the overlapping nature of their trading areas, the Los Angeles and San Francisco exchanges exhibit certain differences. Transactions in dual listings are, for example, rarely divided equally between the 2 exchanges. Tables 26 and 27 indicate that investor interest in regional oil stocks is noticeably greater in southern California than in the Bay Area. This localization of activity is apparently related to the fact that southern California is an important producing area.

A sizable proportion of regional listings may be classified as "home-town" stocks. Such issues are often closely held, and trading is likely to be confined to the locale in which the issuing company's head office is located. For securities of this type, the regional exchange acts in the capacity of a *local* exchange. Combining exchanges will not, at least in the short run, appreciably affect the volume of transactions in local issues. Evidence to support this contention is found in the merger of the Washington and Philadelphia–Baltimore exchanges. Activity in issues which had formerly been traded solely on the Washington Exchange was, in the year following the consolidation, restricted principally to the Washington branch of the Philadelphia–Baltimore Exchange and actually declined in several instances.[28]

Not all exclusive listings need be local issues. Although listed

---

[28] The point might well be made that, because of the increased number of offerings, broker promotion of local issues declined.

solely on the San Francisco Exchange, for example, M.J.M. and M. Oil arouses investor attention in southern California. Since it is not traded on the Los Angeles Exchange, over-the-counter trading in this area is reported to be substantial. For such stocks, unification of the California exchanges might well augment the volume traded on organized exchanges and diminish over-the-counter activity.

Locational factors also account in part for additional diversity of emphasis on the part of the Los Angeles and San Francisco exchanges. The Los Angeles Exchange dually trades in a few stocks listed on the Salt Lake and San Francisco Mining exchanges, as well as those listed on the San Francisco Exchange. The San Francisco Exchange in turn maintains the primary mainland market for several issues listed on the Honolulu Exchange.

BALANCE OF REGIONAL OFFERINGS

Since the trading areas of the California exchanges overlap to a significant extent, dissimilarities among the securities traded on the two exchanges suggest the possibility of improved balance and enlarged activity in the event of merger. With relatively few exceptions, primary San Francisco listings are sparsely distributed among 24 categories. Combination with the Los Angeles Exchange would add 9 regional listings in petroleum, 7 in mining and 8 in other areas.[24] Some 21 of these 24 issues belong to the under-$10 price bracket.

Viewing the consolidation of the California exchanges in terms of its effect upon the San Francisco Exchange, regional offerings are increased to slightly in excess of 100 issues. The balance among regional stocks is not appreciably altered since the primary Los Angeles listings are confined largely to petroleum and mining. Although comparatively few in number, issues traded principally upon the Los Angeles Exchange are extremely active as a rule. Annual volume in 16 securities exceeds 25,000 shares and approaches this level of transactions in 6 other issues. The consequence is that combination significantly augments transactions in regional stocks.

From the standpoint of distribution by price groupings, the balance of offerings by the San Francisco Exchange appears to be adversely affected by union with the Los Angeles Exchange. A

---

[24] In accordance with table 22, dually traded issues are already included among the San Francisco listings.

TABLE 27

COMPARATIVE DAILY TRADING IN DUAL AND MULTIPLE LISTINGS ON THE SAN FRANCISCO, LOS ANGELES, AND AMERICAN EXCHANGES FOR THE TWO-WEEK PERIOD ENDING APRIL 28, 1955

Company	Exchange	Number of shares traded										
		April 15	April 18	April 19	April 20	April 21	April 24	April 25	April 26	April 27	April 28	Total
Bandini Oil	SF	.....	.....	.....	.....	.....	.....	.....	.....	.....	.....	.....
	LA	300	2,230	700	600	600	3,200	200	1,100	100	800	9,830
Bankline Oil	SF	143	.....	.....	.....	.....	200	.....	200	.....	.....	543
	LA	225	.....	200	.....	200	300	.....	250	500	200	1,875
Basin Oil	SF	.....	.....	.....	.....	.....	.....	.....	.....	.....	.....	.....
	LA	1,200	300	.....	100	400	.....	125	1,500	100	720	4,445
Bishop Oil	SF	.....	.....	145	200	300	100	316	.....	.....	.....	1,061
	LA	.....	103	.....	162	183	.....	318	.....	.....	137	903
Bolso Chica Oil	SF	450	300	1,200	600	1,000	800	100	100	.....	.....	4,550
	LA	.....	.....	200	.....	350	100	450	100	.....	250	1,450
Broadway-Hale Stores	SF	200	1,200	30	50	1,537	.....	500	.....	100	160	3,777
	LA	800	20	.....	.....	300	200	.....	400	100	200	2,020
Central Eureka	SF	.....	.....	.....	.....	.....	.....	.....	.....	.....	.....	.....
	LA	.....	.....	.....	.....	.....	.....	.....	.....	.....	.....	.....
Doernbecker Mfg.	SF	.....	.....	.....	.....	.....	.....	.....	.....	.....	.....	.....
	LA	.....	.....	.....	.....	.....	.....	.....	.....	.....	.....	.....
Electrical Prod.	SF	100	.....	.....	.....	.....	.....	.....	.....	.....	.....	100
	LA	.....	.....	220	.....	.....	100	.....	275	250	.....	845
Hancock Oil	SF	150	150	.....	.....	100	100	.....	50	.....	.....	550
	LA	760	647	1,300	1,200	1,035	1,302	.....	1,415	390	716	8,765
Intex Oil	SF	500	.....	.....	.....	.....	100	.....	200	.....	100	900
	LA	.....	.....	500	200	200	1,100	.....	300	200	1,700	4,200
Norris Oil	SF	100	.....	.....	100	100	100	.....	.....	.....	.....	400
	LA	3,300	1,000	1,325	500	500	365	.....	225	200	3,950	11,365

SOURCE: *Wall Street Journal*, Pacific Coast edition.

TABLE 27—Continued

Company	Exchange	\-	\-	\-	\-	Number of shares traded	\-	\-	\-	\-	\-	Total
		April 15	April 18	April 19	April 20	April 21	April 24	April 25	April 26	April 27	April 28	
Holly Development	SF			500	100	100						700
	LA	800		400	200	600			400		1,100	3,500
Occidental Petroleum	SF	542		2,100								2,642
	LA		2,100		200		600					2,900
Pacific Clay Products	SF	100	100									
	LA	100		250	250	250	250					1,100
Pac. Indemnity	SF											
	LA	150		190		100						440
Reserve Oil and Gas	SF		378		1,461	412			142	699	412	3,504
	LA	165			17	100	25		100	100	100	407
So. Calif. Gas (combined)	SF			380	748	100	150	120	100	100	100	1,798
So. Calif. Petroleum	SF	100	220	250		255						825
	LA				200		600	900	200	670	100	2,670
Baldwin Securities	SF											
	LA											
	AM	1,400	1,300	2,000	1,900	1,800	900	1,700	2,600	1,100	700	15,400
Beckman Instruments	SF			50							15	65
	LA	20			100					25	26	171
	AM	1,400	2,100	1,400	500	400	1,100	900	500	900	900	10,100
Calamba Sugar	SF	200							400			600
	LA											
	AM								500	500		1,000
Canadian Atlantic Oil	SF	550		500		300	110	67	500	200		2,227
	LA			100	420				200	200	300	1,220
	AM	1,300	4,800	3,600	2,900	5,600	4,000	1,800	5,100	2,600	4,600	36,300

Source: *Wall Street Journal*, Pacific Coast edition.

TABLE 27—Concluded

Company	Exchange	Number of shares traded										Total
		April 15	April 18	April 19	April 20	April 21	April 24	April 25	April 26	April 27	April 28	
Canadian Homestead	SF	.....	.....	.....	.....	.....	.....	.....	.....	.....	.....	.....
	LA	.....	.....	.....	.....	.....	50	.....	.....	.....	.....	50
	AM	200	100	700	100	100	300	800	400	200	200	3,100
Douglas Oil	SF	.....	200	200	800	600	180	.....	.....	300	25	2,305
	LA	.....	1,800	235	2,430	14,140	6,680	1,525	1,300	1,100	1,250	30,460
	AM	.....	5,700	900	3,000	9,100	10,500	3,500	3,800	3,500	2,600	42,600
Gladding-McBean	SF	.....	100	20	550	.....	.....	100	.....	.....	.....	770
	LA	490	70	50	.....	.....	200	300	100	100	.....	1,310
	AM	.....	400	400	.....	200	.....	600	200	100	.....	1,900
Menasco	SF	400	.....	.....	.....	.....	.....	.....	.....	.....	.....	400
	LA	100	.....	100	.....	.....	100	90	.....	.....	.....	390
	AM	3,300	2,800	1,900	2,300	1,700	1,900	1,600	1,800	1,300	2,000	20,600
Oceanic Oil	SF	.....	1,000	.....	500	200	700	400	2,300	220	.....	5,320
	LA	1,300	600	1,000	330	300	2,650	.....	600	300	.....	7,080
	AM	400	1,100	700	1,200	1,700	1,900	.....	600	400	100	8,100
Pioneer Gold Mines	SF	.....	140	.....	.....	.....	.....	.....	.....	50	.....	190
	LA	.....	.....	.....	.....	.....	.....	.....	.....	.....	.....	.....
	AM	.....	.....	.....	.....	.....	.....	.....	.....	.....	.....	.....
Puget Sound Pulp and Timber	SF	1,100	2,800	100	200	400	100	200	100	.....	.....	5,000
	LA	.....	.....	100	.....	.....	20	.....	.....	.....	.....	120
	AM	.....	.....	.....	.....	.....	.....	.....	.....	.....	.....	1,100
Ryan Aero	SF	.....	.....	1,000	100	200	300	.....	.....	.....	100	1,700
	LA	60	10	200	.....	.....	.....	.....	.....	.....	.....	200
	AM	200	.....	.....	.....	.....	.....	.....	.....	.....	.....	370
Universal Consolidated Oil	SF	14	.....	24	.....	.....	.....	.....	.....	.....	.....	38
	LA	500	.....	.....	.....	250	125	250	.....	169	.....	1,294
	AM	500	500	400	700	900	.....	600	500	.....	400	4,500

SOURCE: *Wall Street Journal*, Pacific Coast edition.

conceivable concern is that the presence of an excessive number of low-priced stocks may occasion undue speculative activity and thereby discourage other and more substantial regional companies from listing their shares. Although not decisive for the Los Angeles Exchange, this consideration may well be crucial in deciding whether or not to include the smaller Western exchanges in the merger. The argument that the usual type of listings on the Salt Lake and San Francisco Mining exchanges is inappropriate material for a major regional exchange has substantial force.

ANTICIPATED BENEFITS

The interrelation of trading areas thus offers several opportunities for augmented activity through consolidation. Improved liquidity through more effective specialist participation and broader distribution of holdings can be expected to awaken investor interest. Enlarged membership in the "new" exchange on a wider geographic base may well expand the area of trading for qualified local issues and diminish over-the-counter trading therein in regions not adequately serviced by the existing membership. To the extent that merger adds to the number of offerings in any given field and therefore to its relative importance, increased attention on the part of brokerage firms is likely to occasion enlarged activity.

Where truly local stocks are concerned, combination of the California exchanges may, in some instances, result in reduced trading. This conclusion follows from two propositions. One is that brokers, given a wider range of offerings, will promote local issues to a lesser degree. The other is that new member firms from other areas will not be interested in exclusively local securities. For such issues, it is entirely possible that over-the-counter markets offer net advantages.

One further positive result of combination, which accrues from the extension of trading areas, now merits consideration. The point has already been made that the fortunes of regional corporations are frequently related to the economic conditions prevailing within the respective trading areas of their securities. As regional markets acquire breadth, the economic strength and diversity of the region encompassed grows; and price and volume fluctuations in regional listings may well bear increasing resemblance to those in national listings.

The matter of Honolulu (and Philippine) listings on the San Francisco Exchange focuses attention upon one possible consequence of coördinated action. Through union of the California exchanges, the West gains an exchange which is initially about double the size of either of its predecessors. Because size and status go hand in hand, the resultant exchange possesses unique prospects for further development by virtue of its location.

In brief, a substantial West Coast exchange might well expand into foreign listings. Such an exchange could conceivably do for the Pacific and South American areas what the American Exchange endeavors to do for the Canadian and European areas. Because of its Spanish background, the California market is perhaps best adapted to the introduction of Mexican and other Latin American issues. Because of its relative proximity, the West Coast market is well suited to the introduction of Philippine, Hawaiian, Australian, and other Pacific area securities.

The concept of an international exchange to parallel the American Exchange cannot be thoroughly treated. Too many intervening steps exist for us to regard it as other than a remote possibilty. The point is raised primarily to demonstrate the range of available alternatives arising as a result of concerted action.

A further aspect of coördinated effort relates to the elimination of interexchange competition. As suggested previously, a given amount of promotional endeavor on the part of a consolidated California exchange might well produce greater results than the same amount divided between the San Francisco and Los Angeles exchanges. The reason is simply that, wherever competing organizations are concerned, a part of the promotional activity is likely to be counteracting.

An analogy can be drawn between this situation and that of corporate advertising policy. When competition is inconsequential, advertising stresses institutional considerations, that is, expansion of the total market for the product. As the significance of competition increases, the emphasis in advertising tends to change to one of maintenance and improvement of relative positions.

Whether interexchange competition is of great importance is debatable. Of far more concern is the competition between regional exchanges and the over-the-counter segment. The elimination of interexchange rivalry is nonetheless of potential benefit.

A final feature of coördinated effort which has been mentioned in connection with size is that the merged exchange has more to offer prospective applicants for listing than do its predecessors. Because of the improved balance in its offerings, the combined exchange can be expected to attract augmented investor interest. In view of the larger number of members, its ability to market securities may well rise. As a consequence of its doubled size relative to either of the former exchanges, publicity is likely to increase.

CONCLUSION

The conclusion is that consolidation provides good possibilities for improving the status of West Coast exchanges. No significant disadvantages appear to exist. The principal problem seems to be one of determining the degree of integration desirable.

VII

Summary and Conclusions

The preceding remarks are based upon the proposition that the truly significant function of regional exchanges is one of providing good markets for regional issues. An alternative function of facilitating entry by regional brokerage firms into the area of national listings appears to possess current relevance. The position is nonetheless taken that the problem of entry can be handled without the complexity introduced by the existence of regional exchanges.

If adequate markets in regional securities are to be maintained by regional exchanges, at least two conditions must obtain. Most important is the matter of exchange status. Regional security exchanges require sufficient prestige to acquire and hold substantial numbers of qualified regional securities and to keep investor interest at a high level. Factors influencing status include size (in terms of both share and dollar volume), balanced offerings of quality stocks, and active, responsible members with substantial financial stakes in the exchange's future.

Of scarcely less consequence than prestige is flexibility. The heterogeneity of regional issues, relative to national listings, necessitates the adaptation of regional exchange procedures to the diverse needs of the trading media. Despite the rigidities imposed by securities regulation, regional exchanges are deemed capable of the requisite adjustments.

EFFECTIVENESS

Although the achievements of regional exchanges exhibit wide variation, their general effectiveness in executing the regional issue function is questionable. Each of the three methods utilized to measure performance suggests deficiencies of one kind or another.

MULTIPLE TRADING

Percentage ratios of regional transactions in multiply traded stocks to total physical volume on regional exchanges average in excess of 50 per cent. This preëminence of multiple trading has two consequences of considerable interest. One is that, given their small size, regional exchanges are likely to possess insufficient bases of active regional listings. The other, and related, item is that the dependence of regional exchanges upon multiple trading diverts attention away from their underlying function.

The objectionable feature of multiple trading is that endeavors to augment transactions in national listings are likely to dominate the policies of regional exchanges. Despite its relatively low multiple trading ratio, the San Francisco Exchange is no exception in this respect.[1] In linking the San Francisco and Los Angeles exchanges by direct wire facilities, the avowed purpose is to facilitate trading in multiply listed issues. In a recent pamphlet publicizing the San Francisco Exchange, emphasis is placed upon the ease with which the corporations whose securities are listed nationally can list regionally.

Since neglect of regional issues and ineffectiveness are undoubtedly closely associated, undue weight by regional exchanges upon multiply trading is fraught with danger. Short-run profits tend to be stressed over longer-run status. This conclusion is not intended to imply that regional trading in national listings should be eliminated. The point is simply that regional volume in multiply traded issues is currently disproportionate.

Several possible justifications for multiple trading have been discussed. The principal one is that the New York Stock Exchange refuses to permit discounts on orders originated by nonmember firms. Others pertain to effect upon total volume, after-hours trading, number of specialists, and indirect subsidization of regional exchanges. None of these considerations is, however, of sufficient force to alter the position taken.

COMPARISON WITH NATIONAL EXCHANGES

With relatively few exceptions, regional exchanges compare unfavorably with their national counterparts. The differential in average daily trading per issue is substantial between national and regional exchanges. A similar result occurs in share turnover. Although the issue is in doubt with respect to trading concentration, the impact of concentration upon regional exchanges is noticeably greater than upon the New York exchanges.

[1] Note that the multiple-trading ratio of the San Francisco Exchange is low only when expressed in terms of share volume.

Despite the observed differences in trading volume, distribution procedures are reasonably standardized among organized exchanges. The evidence nonetheless indicates that procedures which work well for national exchanges are often less effective when adopted by regional exchanges. Because of the limited volume in regional issues, the flow of orders to buy and sell is less likely to be equated on regional exchanges than on the New York exchanges with the result that spreads quoted by regional specialists are relatively high. Failure by regional exchanges to make adjustments which conform to the requirements of regional issues substantiates our conviction that they are neglected in favor of multiply traded issues.

In new listing potential and ability to hold existing listings, regional exchanges are again distinctly inferior to the national exchanges. The primary causes appear to be differences in prestige and conflicting interests confronting member firms. The matter of status is closely related to exchange size, whereas that of conflicting interests arises from the fact that over-the-counter transactions are frequently a major source of income to member firms. The ability to acquire and keep regional listings is highly relevant, for it suggests the direction in which regional exchanges will tend to move.

Variations in trading volume are not the only distinguishing feature. Perhaps the vital consideration in contrasting national and regional exchanges is the nature of the media traded. Regional issues tend to be relatively low priced. In addition, their diversity of quality appears significantly greater than that of national listings. The impression gained from comparing national and regional exchanges is thus one of similar distribution procedures in the face of dissimilar trading media. The inferior performance of regional exchanges implies that alternatives should be explored for changing either one or both of these.

ABSOLUTE CRITERIA

In terms of such absolute criteria as can be formulated, regional exchanges again fall far short of perfection. Their contributions to the salability and price stability of regional issues appear relatively limited. The evidence is, however, inconclusive in the sense that the probable behavior of regional listings in over-the-counter channels, or under other than existing circumstances, is not readily ascertainable.

Objective measures of salability comprise share activity (as associated with relative spreads), trading continuity, and ratios of individual to daily transactions. Employing the 25,000-share minimum set by the Midwest Exchange as a point of departure, it is observed that a substantial number of regional listings are substandard. For these inactive issues relative spreads appear to be somewhat high and to lack consistency.

Nor is trading continuity an outstanding virtue of regional listings if the San Francisco Exchange is any indication. A survey of 25 leading San Francisco listings reveals that almost one-third has orders executed less than three days out of each week, and three-fourths are traded less than four days out of each week. The relative importance of individual orders also seems unduly large for a truly competitive market. Tests of daily trading on the San Francisco Exchange suggest that the over-all ratio of "normal" orders to daily activity per issue is in the neighborhood of 60 per cent.

Largely because the volume of close substitutes for any given regional listing is not known with certainty, conclusions about absorption potential are less definite. The claim-to-income aspect of securities implies that, were it not for imperfect knowledge on the part of investors, a wide variety of substitutes should exist for regional listings. This is not true, however, if the judgment of specialists on the San Francisco Exchange—as reflected in the level and average deviation in quoted spreads—is accepted.

In the matter of price stability, the principal question concerns the degree of market risk associated with regional exchanges. Although precise measurement of market risk is not attempted, certain factors indicate that it is of some importance. Included among the evidences of market risk are smallness of trading volume, sporadic speculative trading, unwillingness of regional companies to list, lack of balance among regional offerings, and variations in historical price-earnings ratios and yields.

Inadequate trading volume on regional exchanges contributes to price instability, as well as affecting salability, for it decreases the likelihood that the flow of orders to purchase regional issues will be equated with the flow of orders to sell. Although not an all-pervasive characteristic of regional exchanges, speculative activity often accentuates the amplitude of price fluctuations in individual issues by disturbing the balance between buy and sell orders. The observed reluctance by regional corporations to list their securities suggests the presence of market risk so far as it reflects the opinion that the distribution procedures of regional exchanges fail to meet the needs of regional issues. Undue concentration in regional listings among a few industries, for example, petroleum in the Los Angeles Exchange, occasions substantial variations in trading volume and reduces the willingness and ability of regional specialists to maintain orderly markets. Finally, variations in price-earnings ratios and yields provide general, but not conclusive, indication of market risk.

Some basis exists for the contention that the risk attached to existing regional listings is of greater consequence than that associated with regional exchanges. To the extent that this is true, primary emphasis should perhaps be placed upon improving the quality of regional listings.

COMPETITION BETWEEN REGIONAL EXCHANGES AND THE OVER-THE-COUNTER SEGMENT

Resolution of the difficulties which confront regional exchanges is complicated by the divided interests of member firms. Member firms deal in both listed and over-the-counter issues and, in many instances, obtain the bulk of their profits from over-the-counter trading. Under such circumstances, serious attempts by regional exchanges to compete with the over-the-counter segment are unlikely to occur.

The basic advantage of the over-the-counter area, as opposed to regional exchanges, is flexibility. Selling effort can be adjusted to fit the requirements of the issue in question. Compensation, in the form of spreads between bid and asked prices, can be varied to provide adequate incentive. Dealer inventories, together with the number of brokerage firms maintaining primary markets, are also adaptable. For regional issues which are characterized by far greater diversity than nationally known and distributed securities, this consideration possesses substantial force.

At least two other factors enhancing the position of the over-the-counter division of the securities market are worthy of mention. One is that all securities are initially distributed over-the-counter. The consequence of this is not only that over-the-counter dealers have the first opportunity to impress their opinion upon corporation executives, but also that companies must take direct action to list their securities.

The second factor is that of disclosure. Corporations whose issues are traded over-the-counter are not required to report to the Securities and Exchange Commission except in connection with new issues. Potentially embarrassing details, such as insider transactions, need not therefore be divulged. From the dealer side, the prices and size of over-the-counter transactions are kept secret. Only bid and offer quotations are publicly reported.

Failure to publicize over-the-counter transactions has important repercussions. Since it curtails certain types of speculative activity, some corporations (especially financial institutions) are influenced not to list their securities. More significant, however, is the fact that imperfect knowledge on the part of investors augments the profit possibilities for over-the-counter dealers and thus increases their resistance to the listing of issues. The absence of disclosure permits variable pricing among brokerage firms and discrimination among customers.

Whether the over-the-counter area can do better than, or even as well as, efficiently operated regional exchanges in creating markets for regional issues which are truly qualified for listing is doubtful. Wherever individual dealers maintain primary markets in numerous over-the-counter issues, only limited attention can be devoted to any single security. Primary dealers receive, in addition, the bulk of their orders from other brokerage firms for the better known over-the-counter stocks. Since spreads between inside and outside prices are roughly equivalent to commission rates, little reason exists for brokerage firms which do not maintain primary markets for the issues in question to favor those securities over listed stocks (unless of course they are nonmember firms).[2] In the absence of substantial improvements in the liquidity of regional issues through over-the-counter trading, it is believed that such securities should be listed in the investor's interest.

PROPOSALS FOR CHANGE

If regional exchanges are to possess longer run significance, certain changes, of both internal and external nature, appear to be in order. In recommending adjustments to the prevailing set-up, emphasis is placed upon matters of exchange status, procedural flexibility, and elimination of legislative discrimination. There is no presumption that the list of proposals presented herein is exhaustive, or that each item is equally vital to the future of regional exchanges. The principal purpose in raising these points is to demonstrate that a variety of possibilities exists.

---

[2] To the extent that regional exchanges offer discounts to nonmember firms which originate business, analogous incentives are provided by regional exchanges.

EXCHANGE STATUS

In order to attract the better-grade regional issues, regional exchanges need to be viewed by the business community as institutions of some stature. The intimate connection between the size and status of regional exchanges suggests the desirability of continued consolidations. A good case can be made for regrouping to the point where three major regional exchanges emerge.

That this process of regrouping is likely to continue is evidenced by the recent plan for establishing the Pacific Coast Stock Exchange. Union of the California exchanges offers excellent potential by virtue of augmented size through consolidation and elimination of intraregional rivalry. It is hoped that complete integration will ultimately be achieved.

Other methods of improving the position of regional exchanges may also be advanced. Active public relations programs oriented to regional companies can produce beneficial effects. At the very least, good-will tours by exchange members and literature addressed to regional corporations, as well as to firms whose issues are nationally listed, merit greater stress. Almost any progressive action by regional exchanges elevates their status, provided it is satisfactorily publicized and efficiently administered.

As a final point, the human factor should not be disregarded. Regional exchanges are associations of securities brokers. Their prominence thus depends upon the activeness, interest, reputation, and position of member firms. With this consideration in mind, attempts (as in the case of the Midwest Exchange) to improve the membership may well bear fruit.

FLEXIBILITY

The failure of distribution procedures employed by regional exchanges to distinguish—in any significant respect—between multiply traded issues and regional listings poses important problems. Whether the proposals presented below provide the requisite adjustments in procedures is subject to debate. What is imperative, however, is that the need for specialized techniques to handle the marketing of regional stocks be recognized and that experimentation be tried along this line.

Existing procedures are presumed to be reasonably well adapted to the marketing of multiply traded securities. Attention is therefore directed solely to the question of regional issues. Aspects considered include, among other things, commission rates, listing criteria, and the specialist function.

By their very nature, regional stocks require greater selling effort than nationally known securities. The average market price per share is, in addition, substantially lower for regional listings than for New York Exchange listings. Unqualified acceptance by regional exchanges of commission rates established by the New York Exchange thus fails to meet the requirements of regional issues. Not only is the incentive of member firms likely to be insufficient in many instances (assuming present commissions to be appropriate for national listings), but also low-priced issues are discriminated against.

The case for experimentation by regional exchanges with dual rate structures appears strong. Initially, the schedule for regional issues might be patterned after the commission rates set by the Canadian exchanges for industrial stocks, with one qualification. This is, that the rates should be based upon the dollar magnitude of individual transactions rather than upon the dollar-size per round-lot. If it is desired (and this is doubtful) to attract issues characterized by high share turnover, lower rates may be established for stocks belonging to such categories as mining and petroleum.[8]

Listing criteria imposed by regional exchanges are reported to be quite flexible. A top official of one exchange does, however, suggest that requirements for listing might well be eased still further. The objective would be to encourage listing before interests are established by over-the-counter dealers.

Although such a proposal has merit as part of a long-range program to augment regional offerings, it does pose problems. Regional exchanges must be equally as willing to take delisting action as they are to permit listing. The reason is simply that reductions in listing standards are likely to increase the quantity of unsuccessful, inactive regional listings. Regional exchanges should also recognize the fact that the risks may be too great in extreme cases for specialists to maintain orderly markets.[4] In these instances, the best solution could well be to eliminate the specialist function entirely (as is done, for example, by the Toronto Exchange). As a

---

[8] This point is unacceptable if the attitude of the business community toward regional exchanges, as well as their character, is adversely affected by the presence of such issues.

[4] Indeed, specialists appear reluctant to take positions in many of the existing regional listings.

final point, it should be observed that the easing of listing criteria will accomplish little by itself.

The matter of adapting the specialist function to the needs at hand has already been mentioned in passing. Since the odd-lot and specialist functions are united at the regional exchange level, differentiation between round-lots and odd-lots should probably be eliminated in the case of regional issues. Arbitrary distinctions of this type are a source of annoyance to investors and do not exist in the over-the-counter area.

One further possibility can be raised in this connection. Member firms, other than specialist firms, might be allowed, and in fact encouraged, to act as principals in regional listings in the interest of orderly markets. Whether this step is realistic of course depends upon the ability of regional exchanges to ensure that such action by member firms will strengthen the specialist's position.

As evidenced by the seat dividend distributed by the San Francisco Exchange and merger activity in the East and Midwest, membership on regional exchanges is characterized by some flexibility. The California exchanges, in addition, offer 25 per cent discounts on commission charges to nonmember firms which originate business. No basis exists for determining the proper number of exchange members. It can, however, be said that discounts to nonmembers originating orders in regional listings should probably be initiated by regional exchanges which presently have no such arrangement, and increased by those which do. The objective is to combat the relative attractiveness of trading in over-the-counter issues by nonmember firms.

The remaining consideration concerns the attention devoted by regional exchanges to individual listings. The prevailing policy of regional exchanges is to restrict information dissemination to the disclosure of actual prices and transactions. Granted that regional exchanges are joint marketing ventures, there is reason to believe that the institutional advertising of regional listings could well be beneficial. The underlying purpose is not to recommend the purchase of particular issues, but rather to acquaint the investing public with the existence of regional trading media.

REMOVAL OF LEGISLATED DISCRIMINATION

Mention has been made of the fact that federal securities regulation distinguishes between listed and over-the-counter issues. Legislated barriers to listing are not to be condoned. The mere occasion of listing does not alter the need for regulation.

The Fulbright bill (S. 2054), presently before the Senate, corrects a major deficiency. It bases requirements for corporate registration and reporting upon asset-size and shareholder numbers rather than upon whether corporate shares are listed. The principal criticism of this bill is that too many categories appear to be exempted.

Additional legislation should perhaps be introduced to provide for the collection and dissemination of information regarding over-the-counter transactions and prices. Criteria for the selection of securities could again be asset-size and shareholder numbers. The intent of such action is clearly to protect the investor and minimize the objections of over-the-counter dealers arising from the presence of vested interests.

Despite the conclusion that regional exchanges leave much to be desired in executing their regional function, it is appropriate to close with an optimistic note. Unless the current wave of corporate mergers continues to an unwarranted extent, reasonable numbers of regional companies are likely to remain in operation. If regional exchanges are truly willing to take progressive action, the possibility of inducing corporate executives to list the issues of their corporations is not necessarily remote.

It is worthy of reiteration that the main task which confronts regional exchanges is likely to be that of convincing exchange members that the servicing of regional issues is an important function. Without active membership participation, the cause appears hopeless.

Appendix

TABLE A-1

COMPARATIVE INDEXES OF STOCK PRICES FOR THE PERIOD 1949 TO 1955
(Base: January, 1949)

Year and month		Moody's Index[a] (125 issues)	Index of San Francisco listings		
			23 firms	9 high-priced	14 low-priced
1949	Jan...............	100.0	100.0	100.0	100.0
	Feb...............	96.0	94.9	96.4	91.1
	Mar...............	99.7	99.5	100.1	98.1
	Apr...............	97.7	100.2	101.8	96.2
	May...............	93.7	96.2	97.6	92.7
	Jun...............	93.8	92.4	94.3	87.3
	Jul...............	99.2	93.3	99.1	92.6
	Aug...............	101.2	101.0	104.7	91.7
	Sep...............	103.9	99.9	105.4	85.9
	Oct...............	107.7	104.4	108.9	93.1
	Nov...............	107.6	104.0	110.7	87.0
	Dec...............	112.8	108.9	116.8	88.7
1950	Jan...............	113.4	109.8	117.4	90.4
	Feb...............	114.1	110.2	117.8	90.7
	Mar...............	116.0	112.1	119.1	94.3
	Apr...............	121.2	112.0	119.5	93.6
	May...............	126.8	116.3	123.8	97.4
	Jun...............	119.8	110.9	118.5	91.4
	Jul...............	121.7	108.3	116.8	86.7
	Aug...............	126.6	115.6	123.3	95.9
	Sep...............	132.2	121.6	133.7	90.8
	Oct...............	133.0	119.7	131.9	88.5
	Nov...............	133.2	120.1	133.7	85.7
	Dec...............	139.0	119.7	131.8	89.1
1951	Jan...............	147.1	131.9	145.4	97.6
	Feb...............	148.0	135.7	149.3	101.0
	Mar...............	145.4	128.6	141.9	94.8
	Apr...............	153.5	129.3	142.8	94.8
	May...............	148.6	126.7	140.4	91.9
	Jun...............	144.0	122.6	134.6	92.0
	Jul...............	153.8	124.3	136.4	93.5
	Aug...............	160.6	129.5	143.3	94.4
	Sep...............	159.8	136.0	152.4	94.2
	Oct...............	155.5	128.9	141.7	96.1
	Nov...............	154.2	129.3	142.8	94.7
	Dec...............	160.1	129.2	143.2	93.4
1952	Jan...............	162.0	128.2	141.4	94.6
	Feb...............	155.3	128.0	141.4	94.1

SOURCE: *Moody's Industrials;* and records of the San Francisco Stock Exchange.
[a] Moody's Index for 125 Industrials, employing month-end weighted average prices.

TABLE A-1—*Continued*

Year and month	Moody's Index[a] (125 issues)	Index of San Francisco listings		
		23 firms	9 high-priced	14 low-priced
Mar..............	163.1	130.7	145.2	93.8
Apr..............	154.7	124.4	138.0	89.6
May.............	158.7	125.8	138.9	92.6
Jun..............	166.1	122.3	135.3	89.4
Jul..............	168.3	124.6	138.8	88.7
Aug.............	165.1	123.3	136.1	90.4
Sep.............	160.9	124.3	139.9	84.4
Oct.............	160.4	118.8	134.7	78.2
Nov.............	168.7	124.7	141.6	81.7
Dec.............	174.5	125.3	142.5	81.6
1953 Jan..............	173.4	127.6	143.3	87.6
Feb.............	170.7	125.1	141.4	83.8
Mar..............	167.5	123.8	138.3	86.6
Apr..............	163.0	122.6	137.7	84.4
May.............	162.7	122.4	137.7	83.6
Jun..............	160.2	118.0	133.2	79.5
Jul..............	164.4	122.1	140.0	76.6
Aug.............	155.0	118.9	137.0	73.1
Sep.............	155.5	118.2	136.7	71.0
Oct.............	163.7	121.0	140.7	70.7
Nov.............	166.0	122.5	143.6	69.9
Dec.............	166.2	122.2	142.3	71.3
1954 Jan..............	175.5	126.6	146.6	75.7
Feb.............	176.8	127.6	147.1	78.1
Mar..............	184.5	132.5	152.9	80.5
Apr..............	195.8	134.5	156.1	79.7
May.............	199.5	139.7	163.6	78.8
Jun..............	205.9	139.7	163.4	79.2
Jul..............	212.1	151.6	177.3	86.3
Aug.............	209.2	146.3	171.6	81.9
Sep.............	222.0	152.9	178.2	88.4
Oct.............	217.8	152.2	175.7	92.5
Nov.............	239.5	162.7	189.1	95.5
Dec.............	249.4	163.0	184.4	108.7

SOURCE: *Moody's Industrials;* and records of the San Francisco Stock Exchange.
[a] Moody's Index for 125 Industrials, employing month-end weighted average prices.

TABLE B-1

RELATIVE SPREADS ON PRIMARY SAN FRANCISCO LISTINGS FOR THREE TRADING DAYS[a]

Price range (dollars)	Issue	Symbol	1954 trading activity	Percentage ratios of spreads to closing bids as of:		
				Mar. 15, 1955	Dec. 15, 1954	Sept. 15, 1954
0–5	Central Eureka.......	CU	286,032	1	5	6
	Canadian Homestead..	CHO	187	2	36	68
	Blair Holdings........	BLR	813,112	3	3	3
	Philippine Tel.........	PHI	96,457	3	7	2
	Westates (Com).......	WPT	221,417	3	9	4
	Calamba Sugar........	CEE	9,717	4	8	8
	Doernbecker Mfg.....	DB	75,749	4	2	2
	Pac. Oil and Gas......	POC	53,735	4	13	6
	Utah-Idaho Sugar.....	UIS	9,541	4	13	6
	Douglas Oil...........	DOU	24,919	5	13	14
	Idaho-Maryland.......	IM	423,921	5	8	4
	Norris Oil............	NRO	8,625	5	20	40
	Atok Big-Wedge......	ATK	90,017	6	6	11
	Federated Petrol......	FEP	7,258	6	19	14
	Oceanic Oil...........	OCN	258,053	6	7	4
	Bandini Petrol........	BDI	13,731	7	3	8
	Onomea Sugar........	ON	929	7	4	27
	Cypress Abbey........	CYP	7,238	8	13	18
	Bolsa Chica Oil.......	BCO	40,971	10	4	3
	Eureka Corp. Ltd......	EKA	13,203	11	7	29
	Palmer Stendel Oil.....	PAL	713,845	11	4	3
	Holly Dev............	HDV	27,892	13	4	17
	New Park Mining......	NKM	3,035	17	9	25
	Lyons-Magnus (B).....	LYB	3,575	18	18	30
	Occidental Petrol.....	OP	21,957	25	29	50
	San Mauricio Min......	SAN	1,445,376	25	20	20
	Mindanao Mother Lode	MD	1,598,852	33	33	25
	Alaska-Juneau Gold ...	AJ	3,313	37	23	4
	Vica.................	VI	1,755	50	100	b
	Pig'n Whistle.........	PGNZ	3,705	65	73	40
	Eureka (Wts).........	EKA–WTS	650	100	67	100
	Clayton Silver Mines...	CSM	....	b	b	b
	El Paso Nat. Gas......	EIG	23,178	c	c	2
	Pacific Clay...........	PC	200	c	c	c
	Union Oil (Cal) Prfd...	UCLQ	....	c	2	2
5–10	Westates Prfd.........	WPTQ	148,730	1	1	2
	Pac Coast Agg.........	PAG	123,761	3	2	2
	Canadian Atlantic.....	CAT	88,917	4	4	5
	Intex Oil.............	INX	48,995	4	5	1
	Menasco Mfg.........	MEN	64,075	4	5	5
	Merrill Pet Ltd........	(–)	Not listed	5	N.L.	N.L.

TABLE B-1—*Continued*

Price range (dollars)	Issue	Symbol	1954 trading activity	Percentage ratios of spreads to closing bids as of:		
				Mar. 15, 1955	Dec. 15, 1954	Sept. 15, 1954
5–10	El Dorado Oil.........	ELW	186,199	6	3	6
	Yellow Cab...........	CAB	17,219	6	6	4
	Bailey Selburn Oil.....	BSOA	870	7	11	5
	Paauhau Sugar........	PAS	1,570	13	21	17
	Honokoa Sugar........	HOK	1,750	b	12	3
	Hutchinson Sugar.....	HTS	335	b	b	b
10–30	Gen'l Paint 2nd Pfd....	GPNQ II	3,761	1	18	19
	Hawaiian Pineapple....	HIP	88,895	1	1	2
	Hancock Oil Pfd.......	HCKQ	5,660	2	2	2
	DiGiorgio (B).........	DGB	34,748	2	2	6
	Gen'l Paint...........	GPN	40,175	2	4	2
	Oahu Sugar...........	OU	12,436	2	2	6
	Pacific Petrol.........	PPE	79,979	2	2	5
	Super Mold...........	SUM	19,476	2	2	8
	Union Sugar..........	USC	28,129	2	2	2
	Western Dept. St......	WS	62,836	2	1	1
	Beckman Inst.........	BEC	3,992	3	4	4
	Bishop Oil...........	BIS	32,921	3	2	2
	Byron Jackson........	BJC	9,577	3	2	4
	Colorado Fuel, Iron....	CF	16,221	3	1	4
	Marchant............	MRC	113,673	3	2	2
	Broadway-Hale.......	BRD	26,482	4	2	2
	Hunt Foods...........	HFD	10,666	4	3	4
	Victor Equipt.........	VE	38,593	4	4	2
	Calaveras Cement.....	CAC	68,175	5	2	1
	DiGiorgio (A).........	DGA	10,086	5	6	6
	Ewa Plantation.......	EWA	7,072	5	3	2
	Gladding McBean.....	GLD	11,751	5	8	10
	S/W Fine Foods.......	SWF	54,232	5	2	4
	Bankline Oil..........	BKL	15,190	6	10	9
	Gen'l Paint Pfd.......	GPNQ	6,825	6	6	19
	Meier and Frank......	MRF	8,258	7	5	7
	So Calif Petrol........	SPT	43,578	7	4	7
	Dorr-Oliver Com......	(–)	Not listed	8	N.L.	N.L.
	Emsco Mfg............	EDR	....	8	18	5
	No. Amer. Invest......	NI	5,733	8	4	4
	Yellow Cab Prfd.......	CABQ	535	8	11	7
	No. Am. Invest. Pfd....	NIQ	7,593	9	2	b
	Calif. Ink.............	CIC	15,537	11	4	0
	Railway Equip........	RE	5,870	12	5	6
	Foster, Kleiser Pfd.....	FKLQ	432	b	b	b
	No. Am. Inv. 5½ Pfd...	NIQ5½	6,357	b	b	b
	Wailuku Sugar........	WAL	50	b	b	b

TABLE B-1—*Concluded*

Price range (dollars)	Issue	Symbol	1954 trading activity	Percentage ratios of spreads to closing bids as of:		
				Mar. 15, 1955	Dec. 15, 1954	Sept. 15, 1954
30 and over	Pac Tel Pfd..........	PACQ	528	0	1	2
	Anglo Calif Nat'l......	ANB	59,105	1	0	1
	Archer Daniels Midlands	ADM	708	1	2	3
	Clorox Chemical.......	CXC	14,007	1	1	2
	P. T and T............	TAC	9,230	1	1	1
	So Calif Gas..........	SOAQ	1,184	1	2	2
	Union Oil.............	UCL	109,438	1	1	1
	Russ Bldg Pfd.........	RBCQ	2,218	N.L.	1	22
	Emp-Capwell.........	EMC	49,623	2	1	2
	Kern Co. Land........	KCY	36,440	2	1	2
	Pac Western Oil.......	PWO	13,214	2	1	2
	Warren Petrol........	WRN	3,792	2	2	4
	Dorr-Oliver Pfd......	(–)	Not listed	3	N.L.	N.L.
	Honolulu Oil.........	HNU	9,752	3	3	1
	Wells Fargo..........	WF	245	3	4	3
	Le Tourneau..........	LTU	....	4	4	7
	Roos Bros............	ROB	2,542	4	5	7
	Univ. Consol. Oil......	UCO	2,326	4	3	5
	Reserve Oil...........	RVO	4,432	5	c	c
	Hancock Oil..........	HCK	60,874	6	2	3
	Leslie Salt...........	LE	10,407	10	3	5
	Weill and Co.........	RWE	474	12	b	20
	Railway Equip't Pfd...	REQ	2,192	19	b	3
	DiGiorgio Pfd........	DGQ	1,253	b	10	b
	Crocker First........	CFN	2,180	b	4	6

SOURCE: San Francisco Stock Exchange, *Daily Summary of Transactions.*
a New York Exchange listings excluded. Included are dual listings with the Los Angeles Exchange and some multiple listings with the American Exchange.
b No asked price.
c Neither price given.

TABLE A-2

COMPARATIVE INDEX OF STOCK PRICES FOR THE YEAR 1946
(Base: January, 1946)

1946 month	Moody's Index (125 common)	Index of San Francisco listings (sample of 21)
Jan.	100.0	100.0
Feb.	94.3	94.4
Mar.	99.4	99.2
Apr.	104.1	100.7
May	107.0	107.9
Jun.	102.7	99.5
Jul.	100.7	95.0
Aug.	93.5	88.9
Sep.	84.8	79.0
Oct.	84.7	77.9
Nov.	84.1	75.9
Dec.	88.0	77.1

SOURCE: Same as table A-1.

TABLE A-3

COMPARATIVE INDEXES OF STOCK PRICES FOR THE PERIOD 1937 TO 1939
(Base: June, 1937)

Year and month		Moody's Index (125 common)	Index of San Francisco listings (sample of 21)
1937	Jun.	100.00	100.0
	Jul.	108.67	107.2
	Aug.	103.65	104.6
	Sep.	89.24	89.3
	Oct.	79.94	77.5
	Nov.	70.9	66.0
	Dec.	68.2	59.9
1938	Jan.	69.9	64.4
	Feb.	74.4	65.0
	Mar.	56.4	50.1
	Apr.	64.1	55.6
	May	60.9	54.4
	Jun.	76.4	65.2
	Jul.	82.0	68.0
	Aug.	79.8	63.7
	Sep.	81.0	61.2
	Oct.	85.9	67.2
	Nov.	83.8	63.4
	Dec.	87.5	59.2

SOURCE: Same as table A-1.

Appendix

TABLE B-2

RATIOS OF AVERAGE DEVIATIONS TO AVERAGE RELATIVE SPREADS
FOR SAN FRANCISCO LISTINGS
(in per cent)

Price range (dollars)	Issue (symbol)	(1) Average relative spread	(2) Average deviation	Ratio of 2 to 1
0–5	CU....................	4.0	2.0	50.0
	CHO..................	35.3	22.0	62.0
	BLR..................	3.0	–o–	–o–
	PHI..................	4.0	2.0	50.0
	WPT..................	5.3	2.4	45.0
	CEE..................	6.7	1.1	16.0
	DB...................	2.7	.9	33.0
	POC..................	7.7	3.6	47.0
	UIS..................	7.7	3.6	47.0
	DOU..................	10.7	3.8	36.0
	IM...................	5.7	1.1	19.0
	NRO..................	21.7	12.2	56.0
	ATK..................	7.7	2.2	29.0
	FEP..................	13.0	4.7	36.0
	OCN..................	5.7	1.1	19.0
	BDI..................	6.0	2.0	33.0
	ON...................	12.7	9.6	76.0
	CYP..................	13.0	3.3	25.0
	BCO..................	5.7	2.9	51.0
	EKA..................	15.7	8.9	57.0
	PAL..................	6.0	3.3	55.0
	HDV..................	11.3	4.9	43.0
	NKM..................	17.0	5.3	31.0
	LYB..................	22.0	5.3	24.0
	OP...................	34.7	10.2	29.0
	SAN..................	21.7	2.3	11.0
	MD...................	30.3	3.6	12.0
	AJ...................	21.3	11.6	54.0
	VI...................	75.0	25.0	33.0
	PGNZ.................	59.3	13.2	22.0
	EKA–WTS.............	89.0	14.7	17.0
	ELG..................	1.0	1.0	100.0
	UCLQ.................	2.0	–o–	–o–
5–10	WPTQ................	1.3	.4	31.0
	PAG..................	2.3	.4	17.0

SOURCE: Table B-1.

TABLE B-2 (*Continued*)

Price range (dollars)	Issue (symbol)	(1) Average relative spread	(2) Average deviation	Ratio of 2 to 1
5–10	CAT...................	4.3	.4	9.0
	INX...................	3.3	1.6	48.0
	MEN...................	4.7	.4	8.0
	ELW...................	5.0	1.3	26.0
	CAB...................	5.3	.9	17.0
	BSOA..................	7.7	2.2	29.0
	PAS...................	17.0	2.7	16.0
	HOK...................	7.5	4.5	60.0
10–30	GPNQ II...............	12.7	7.8	61.0
	HIP...................	1.3	.4	31.0
	HCKQ.................	2.0	–o–	–o–
	DGB...................	3.3	1.8	55.0
	GPN...................	2.7	.9	33.0
	OU....................	3.3	1.8	55.0
	PPE...................	3.0	1.3	43.0
	SUM...................	4.0	2.7	68.0
	USC...................	2.0	–o–	–o–
	WS....................	1.3	.4	31.0
	BEC...................	3.7	.4	11.0
	BIS...................	2.7	.6	22.0
	BJC...................	3.0	.7	23.0
	CF....................	2.7	1.1	41.0
	MRC...................	2.3	.4	18.0
	BRD...................	2.7	.9	33.0
	HFD...................	3.7	.4	11.0
	VE....................	3.3	.9	27.0
	CAC...................	2.7	.9	33.0
	DGA...................	5.7	.4	7.0
	EWA...................	3.3	1.1	33.0
	GLD...................	7.7	1.8	23.0
	SWF...................	3.7	1.1	30.0
	BKL...................	8.3	1.6	19.0
	GPNQ..................	10.3	5.8	56.0
	MRF...................	6.3	.9	14.0
	SPT...................	6.0	1.3	22.0
	EDR...................	10.3	5.1	50.0
	NI....................	5.3	1.8	34.0
	CABQ..................	8.7	1.6	18.0

SOURCE: Table B-1.

TABLE B-2 (*Concluded*)

Price range (dollars)	Issue (symbol)	(1) Average relative spread	(2) Average deviation	Ratio of 2 to 1
10–30	NIQ..................	5.5	3.5	64.0
	CIC..................	7.5	3.5	47.0
	RE...................	7.7	2.9	38.0
30 and over	PACQ................	1.0	.7	70.0
	ANB.................	.7	.4	57.0
	ADM.................	2.0	.7	35.0
	CXC.................	1.3	.4	31.0
	PAC..................	1.0	—o—	—o—
	SOAQ................	1.7	.4	24.0
	UCL.................	1.0	—o—	—o—
	KBCQ...............	11.5	10.5	91.0
	EMC.................	1.7	.4	24.0
	KCY.................	1.7	.4	24.0
	PWO.................	1.7	.4	24.0
	WRN................	2.7	.9	33.0
	HNOU...............	2.3	.9	39.0
	WF..................	3.3	.4	12.0
	LTU.................	5.0	1.3	26.0
	ROB.................	5.3	1.1	21.0
	UCO.................	4.0	.7	18.0
	HCK.................	3.7	1.6	43.0
	LE...................	6.0	2.7	45.0
	RWE................	16.0	8.0	50.0
	REQ.................	11.0	8.0	73.0
	CFN.................	5.0	1.0	20.0
	WF..................	1.5	.5	33.0

SOURCE: Table B-1.

TABLE C-1

**PERCENTAGE RATIOS OF DAYS-NOT-TRADED TO TOTAL TRADING DAYS FOR SELECTED
SAN FRANCISCO ISSUES DURING THE YEARS 1937, 1938, AND 1946**

Issue	Percentage ratios		
	1937[a]	1938[b]	1946[c]
Anglo-California	51.7	62.2	25.8
Atlas	47.7	55.2	....
Blair Holdings	....	....	7.0
California Cotton	79.0	84.9	....
Calaveras	....	....	78.1
Consolidated Chemical	67.0	....	....
Central Eureka	....	....	25.8
Di Giorgio	60.8	75.6	....
Dominguez	....	....	15.9
El Dorado	88.1	94.0	48.3
Emporium Capwell	41.5	53.8	27.2
General Paint	56.3	55.9	48.7
Golden State	25.6	33.8	20.2
Hale Brothers	72.7	83.9	....
Hawaiian Pineapple	40.3	52.8	29.1
Honolulu Oil	56.8	55.2	....
Hunt	79.5	86.6	....
Idaho-Maryland	....	....	32.1
Index Oil	....	....	65.6
Leslie Salt	75.6	85.3	....
Magnin, I.	79.0	77.6	....
Marchant	32.4	54.2	73.8
Matson	....	....	20.9
Menasco	....	....	14.9
MJM and M Oil	....	....	41.1
North American Oil	42.0	59.5	....
Pacific Coast Aggregates	....	....	32.5
S and W Fine Foods	....	....	56.3
Soundview	11.9	22.7	....
Union Sugar	42.6	70.9	....
Westates Com	....	....	46.0
Westates Pfd	....	....	24.8
Western Dept Stores	....	....	43.4
West Pipe	54.5	71.2	....

SOURCE: Records of the San Francisco Stock Exchange.
[a] Last seven months of 1937, covering 176 trading days.
[b] 299 trading days.
[c] 302 trading days.

Index

www.ingramcontent.com/pod-product-compliance
Lightning Source LLC
Chambersburg PA
CBHW021712210326
41599CB00013B/1626